Silas Wright Burt, Edward L. Berthoud

**The Rocky Mountain gold regions**

Silas Wright Burt, Edward L. Berthoud

**The Rocky Mountain gold regions**

ISBN/EAN: 9783337717889

Printed in Europe, USA, Canada, Australia, Japan

Cover: Foto ©ninafisch / pixelio.de

More available books at **www.hansebooks.com**

# THE
# ROCKY MOUNTAIN
# GOLD REGIONS

CONTAINING SKETCHES OF

Its History, Geography, Botany, Geology,

MINERALOGY AND GOLD MINES,

AND THEIR PRESENT OPERATIONS.

WITH A COMPLETE HISTORY OF THE MILLS FOR REDUCING QUARTZ NOW OPERATING.

ILLUSTRATED BY TWO MAPS.

BY S. W. BURT AND E. L. BERTHOUD.

DENVER CITY, J. T.:
PUBLISHED BY THE ROCKY MOUNTAIN NEWS PRINTING CO.
1861.

The authors propose to make this publication periodical, and a complete record of Quartz Mining operations, with full descriptions of such discoveries, inventions and improvements as may affect the Mining interests. They will also include such further information in regard to the Natural History of the country as may be obtained, and to all matters touching the general interests—among which they will give special attention to the collection of data affecting the location of the Pacific Railroad through the Mountain Range.

B. & B.

GOLDEN CITY, J. T., January, 1861.

# PREFATORY.

The inception of this work originated in the desire of the authors to obtain reliable statistics in regard to the Quartz Mining in the Rocky Mountains for their own personal purposes. But finding public information on the subject to be vague and erroneous, they were induced to issue a circular to the mill-owners, explanatory of their design, and proposing a set of queries embracing all the necessary information required. The following extract from that circular will illustrate their purpose.

"The auriferous Quartz Mining, in the Rocky Mountains,
"presents the anomaly of a large investment of capital and
"labor in a branch of industry, which in its general aspects
"is entirely foreign to the experience of most of those en-
"gaged in it, and in its special adaptation to the locality and
"specific qualities of the rocks operated upon, may be con-
"sidered a novel and unprecedented undertaking. But that
"characteristic American enterprise, that no sooner discov-
"ers an unexplored source of wealth than it hastens to de-
"velope it, has already expended here an amount of capital
"and industry, within a limited period, hitherto unparalleled.
"It yet remains a matter of pure experiment, and though
"many mills are eminently successful, the very diversity of
"machinery proves that the standard is yet to be established

"With a view of hastening the solution of this important question and also collecting such statistics as will illustrate the extensive scale of operations already entered into, we have taken the liberty of addressing to you the annexed queries."

Subsequently each of the mills was visited and examined by the authors. The catalogue of the mills will be found full and complete up to date of publication. The fact that no satisfactory information in regard to the Natural History of the country had yet been published, induced the authors to insert here the fruits of their individual observations made during a residence of three months. Though their views may appear crude and imperfect, since their time has been too fully occupied by professional labors to permit thorough examination, they trust they will be received leniently, as a small contribution to the scanty information extant in regard to this country. They have also added the first detailed map of the Quartz Mining Region yet published.*

We trust our little work will prove of benefit to those engaged in mining, by directing their attention to the magnitude of the interests involved, and by consolidating and rendering available all the knowledge obtained to this time. Our fellow citizens at the East will obtain by its perusal some adequate idea of the extraordinary resources of our new region, and food for admiration in the perseverance and energy of its inhabitants, who have transported across a desert of 500 miles over a hundred steam engines and other massive machinery, and are now pursuing their laborious occupations in the heart of the Rocky Mountains. Where two years ago the yell of the panther or war cry of the Indian alone broke the solitude, the steam whistle now awakens a thousand echoes, proclaiming

---

* Through the suggestion of A. D. Richardson, Esq., we have added a sketch of the routes to the Gold Region, similar to the one published last year from his drawings and observations, and which had an extraordinary newspaper circulation of 400,000 copies.

the existence of an industrious and peaceable population in spite of all the discouragements of a pioneer life, rendered yet more formidable by the culpable neglect of the general government.

# HISTORICAL.

When it was that the first white man explored the region of country between the Arkansas and the North Platte, and from the South Platte to the Great Basin, is very difficult if not impossible to determine. The Spaniards in Mexico are the first who pretended to give to the world an account of these regions. About 1540-50, a large expedition organized in Mexico and under a Spanish officer, Vasquez de Coronada, penetrated into what is now Arizona, New Mexico and Utah, and probably even farther north into what is now Kansas. He is the first, that made known to the world that here animals abounded whom he described as "*bueyes con una giba*" or oxen with a hump upon their backs, (Buffalo). As the localities he describes, from his imperfect knowledge of geography and the unknown regions he was exploring, are now difficult to identify, we may suppose without any great stretch of imagination that he visited the vast prairie country near the Arkansas River. Other expeditions of the French and Spaniards afterwards attempted to explore the country which to the north-west, the Indians represented as abounding in gold and silver, but the vast prairies, the barren deserts and hostile savages rendered their attempts abortive. About 1760-70; Father ESCALENTE, a Jesuit missionary, travelled from New Mexico in a northerly direction and penetrated by the Rio Colorado to Great Salt Lake, and wrote an account of his journey. Whether he visited the Parks or crossed the Snowy Range by the Coocheetope Pass, or by the Pass near Long's Peak, is not clearly known. In 1802-3 the U. S. Government, desirous of examining and knowing the geological features of the region immediately contiguous to the boundaries agreed upon between Spain, the United States and the Province of Louisana, sent a zealous young officer, Lieut. ZEBULON PIKE (afterwards killed at Kingston, Canada,) to explore the head of the Arkansas and Canadian Rivers. Proceeding with his party by the Osage and the Neosho Rivers, in what is now Southern Kansas, he crossed the last stream to the Arkansas and explored that river and the Canadian and Rio del Norte regions, and discovered the high Peak which bears his name and has recently become famous as the popular title of the whole gold region. He then crossed from the Arkansas to the head of the Rio Grande, where being lost, and in an unknown country, he was finally captured and taken prisoner by the Spaniards, but was shortly afterwards released. From this time till 1820, the U. S. Government took no steps towards exploring this part of the Territories; in that year a large expedition under Major LONG, Top. Eng'rs., was sent via the Missouri and Platte Rivers to the Rocky Mountains to make a complete and accurate sketch of the Geography, Natural History and resources of the country. Accompanied by naturalists, scientific men and all the necessaries for these purposes, with Dr. JAMES J. B. SAY and others, he made a complete examination of the Platte, South Platte and Mountain Ranges, and on his return gave us the first full account we have of Western Kansas and Nebraska. In view of the distance and unknown character of the country, compared to the facilities of the present time, it is an exceedingly valuable report, and on it, for twenty-five years, was based all our knowledge of the vast region between the Missouri and the Great Basin.

About 1842-5, Government desirous of still further extending our knowledge of the country included between the Missouri and the Pacific and bordering on California, sent out two expeditions under Capt. J. C. FREMONT; who, each time starting from Ft. Leavenworth and from Kansas City, explored the Kansas, Republican, Smoky Hill and Solomon's Forks, the Arkansas, North and South Platte and the Boiling Spring Rivers, and the North, South and Middle Parks. In his rapid surveys he traced the course of the South Platte, Cherry Creek, Cache la Poudre and other small streams, but except in the South Park did not traverse the mountains in the neighborhood of Long's Peak. This expedition, which rendered the Geography of this part of the Rocky Mountains comparatively well known, is the authority for all the maps of this region yet published. Since Capt. FREMONT's last expedition, several explorations of the country north and south of the region between 41° and 38° 30. North Latitude have been made but without extending our knowledge of the discussed region. We would, however, refer to the journal of an enterprising New Englander, who about the winter of 1834-5 visited the western branches of the South Platte, Vasquez Fork and Boulder Creek and the region around Long's Peak. He also visited the country now included in the Gregory, Russell, Nevada and Clear Creek mining districts, but as it was in winter, the golden treasures he then passed over lay bound up in ice and frost. His motive for penetrating the mountains was derived from the report of the Indians that there existed a great interior basin, which abounded in meadows, open glades and countless game.

Such was the knowledge of this region, possessed by the world at large up to 1858, if we except a few solitary trappers and traders who lived for years at the foot of the mountains, or some adventurous Californians who *prospected* for gold on the North and South Plattes, and finding it in several places, attempted to return and open the new Gold Region;

but the remote and lonely situation of the mountains and the difficulty experienced in obtaining credence in their discoveries prevented their return. Capt. STANSBURY, in 1849, was shown a piece of quartz obtained S. W. of Fort Bridger, but the fact was unnoticed in the heat of California excitement. In 1858, a party of men from the Cherokee nation, composed of Georgians and others, and a party from Lawrence, Kansas, prospected during the summer from Northern New Mexico to near the Cache la Poudre river, and when in the fall of '58, the companies for want of success or otherwise had nearly disbanded, they met at the confluence of the South Platte and Cherry Creek, (now Denver). Here finding good "prospects" of gold in these streams, and joined by others from Eastern Kansas and Nebraska, allured by the reports of those returning, they prepared to remain during the winter.

The succeeding spring, (1859,) found them busily mining and prospecting the country in every direction, and as it was now well known in the Eastern States that gold or its "color" could be found on the Platte and its tributaries, a large emigration started from the Missouri River, and which, in the suffering encountered on the Plains and in results at the mines, produced a painful feeling of disappointment in the public mind. Even the miners themselves became disheartened, both by the scarcity of provisions and the lateness of the season, and harassed and threatened by discouraged emigrants, many returned across the inhospitable desert; Denver became almost deserted and even the most sanguine began to loose faith. At this opportune moment, the discovery of the Gregory Mines, on May 18th, on a small branch of North Clear Creek, relieved the scanty population of Denver from the apprehensions of total destruction threatened by the emigrants, who declared they had been induced by *humbug* reports to visit the Rocky Mountains for ulterior purposes, and that the gold was a myth. The rush to the Gregory district became immense, and soon the further discovery of

Russell's, Nevada, Eureka, Lake and other gulches, and later of rich auriferous quartz veins, established beyond doubt the fact that a new source of gold was presented to the world. Cherry Creek and South Platte were soon abandoned for these more promising regions, and the revival of public confidence encouraged enterprise in every direction. Since then the area of gold-producing country has been steadily increasing, and along Clear Creek, Boulder in the South Park, at the head of the South Platte, at Tarryall and Graball, and on the head-waters of the Blue river, rich gulch mines were discovered in 1859. During the winter and spring of 1859-60, those remaining in the mining region prospected over a large area, discovered new quartz veins and extracted a large amount of quartz, to be ground by the mills expected from the East during the ensuing summer. The immense amount of labor performed during the previous winter was one of the most interesting objects to the new comer this spring, and he viewed the honey-combed mountains with an oppressive astonishment when he recollected that not a year had elapsed since the white man first came with pick and shovel. In April, 1860, the reported discovery of rich mines on the Arkansas drew thither a large amount of miners, and their continued success attracted a large proportion of the year's emigration. Though very rich gulch mines have been thus far discovered, we can as yet hear of no quartz veins, probably because no effort has been made to explore for them. The Middle Park also has been found rich in gold, but the remoteness of the locality and cold temperature have been thus far a great obstacle to mining enterprise. The mines of Boulder Creek, a branch of St. Vrain River, were discovered in the winter and spring of 1859 and the gulch diggings at Deadwood and Jefferson produced a very superior quality of gold, but in quantities too small to encourage a continuance of mining. The quartz veins however, at Gold Hill and vicinity of Utilla Creek and near South Boulder, have proved exceedingly rich and quite as promising as any in the Clear Creek district. There is no doubt but that the area of the gold-field will be greatly extended this year, as many prospecting parties are engaged in different directions.

# GEOGRAPHICAL.

The gold region of the Rocky Mountains, which besides Western Kansas, embraces part of Nebraska and Utah Territories, extends from 105° Long. W. of Greenwich to about 107° W. and from Lat. 30° to 41° N., and this comprises only the portion thus far examined and subject to indefinite extension by future discoveries. The area thus bounded contains not only a part of the Mountains, but also a large portion of the so-termed Great American Desert, and prior to 1858 was all considered as a not coveted residence for truculent Indians and wild animals but was deprived by inspection of many of its terrors, and contains an actual population of 45,000 souls.* This portion of the great Cordillera, which beginning at the Sierra del Fuego in the Southern Hemisphere, extends all along the west coast of South America and thence through North America to Mt. St. Elias and the McKenzie River, is made more remarkable here by several interesting and note-worthy peculiarities. The main Snowy Range, which in Kansas, is a continuation of the Sierra San Juan, keeps a due north course up to about Lat. 39° N., here running easterly

---

* This does not include the Indian tribes, and is believed to be within bounds. The decennial census now being compiled, will probably give very accurate and valuable results, and information in regard to number and origin of our present population.

some distance and continuing also in its original northern course, it feeds from its eternal snows, the head waters of the Arkansas, the North and South Platte and the Rio Grande del Norte, whose waters finally reach the Gulf of Mexico; while from its western slope emerge the Grand, Blue, Green and San Juan Rivers, all tributaries to the majestic Colorado of the west. Thus in a mountain range of only 3° of Lat. in extent, by 2° of Long. in width, is the origin of four of the largest rivers in the world, whose waters parting at the Snowy Range seek an outlet in the two great Oceans. Another singular feature of this portion of the mountain range are the North, Middle and South Parks, which are interior meadows or prairies watered by beautiful streams and surrounded by snowy peaks and craggy mountains in every direction, except where the North and South Platte and Blue rivers leave their peaceful and sheltered bosom, and through deep, rugged and precipitous canons force their way in boiling torrents and cataracts. A journey of eleven miles will take the tourist from the head waters of the South Platte to the head of Blue River, and another day's travel crosses another high range and brings him to the Arkansas. It is on the head waters of all the streams mentioned, that the gold region is situated and in districts generally deriving names from the various waters. The Snowy Range that separates South from Middle Park runs in its easterly course from 40 to 60 miles towards the South Platte, then turning north it continues to Long's Peak, and then tending to N. W. and W. finally returns to its original course on the west side of the North Park.

Entering the South Platte some five miles north of Denver is Vasquez Fork or Clear Creek, and which is a beautiful stream of 100 to 150 feet wide and fed by an hundred tributaries from the Snowy Range, flows between mountain meadows and rocky heights, until forcing its way through a canon it emerges into the Plains and between willow-fringed banks it seeks its outlet. Passing through the canon of one and a half miles, we easily ascend the stream until at a distance of twenty miles from Golden City, which is situated at its exit from the mountains, we reach the diggings known as Grass Valley, Illinois and Soda Creek Bars, and one mile above these are Chicago, Payne's and Spanish Bars. Five miles below these last the main stream receives an accession called North Clear Creek, and about four miles above their junction the latter is divided into numerous branches, well known as Russell's, Missouri, Chase's and Gregory's Gulches, and which in their turn are fed by smaller tributaries such as Eureka, Nevada, Spring, Lake and other Gulches. This region includes the most populous and thus far, the richest gold bearing country, and here the largest amount of capital and labor has been invested in Quartz Mining. The two great branches of Vasquez Fork, known as South and North Clear Creeks have their origin at the very base of the mountain range; the former in a westerly direction from the mouth, and the latter near the "New Diggings" not far south of the Pass near Long's Peak, leading to the Middle Park and the head of the Blue River.

To the north and in the immediate vicinity of Long's Peak we find Left-Hand or Utilla Creek on which, about eight or ten miles from where it emerges from the mountains, is situated the second great Quartz Mining Region, known also as the Boulder District.

The fall of Clear Creek, from the mines to the Platte, though rapid is regular: at Golden City the fall is 48 feet per mile, and in the canon it probably reaches 75 feet per mile, but when the canon is passed the rise is much less, and regular to near the foot of the Snowy Range, by either the main branch, Chicago Creek or Fall River. It is not presumption to say that a railroad could be built up this creek to within four miles of the Snowy Range, with no grades exceeding 90 feet per mile, and in many places as low as 50 feet per mile. The authors of this sketch have examined the stream for twenty-five miles from the valley, and have found no obstacles more difficult than those that have been overcome on the New York and Erie, on the Delaware River, or the Ohio and Baltimore Railroads; and it is firmly believed that by ascending the main stream and probably one of its tributaries that a Pass can be found to the Middle Park in a direct line from St. Joseph to Leavenworth, by means of a tunnel not exceeding 2½ miles long. The successful construction of a railroad from the great valley to the forks of Clear Creek, and thence to Gregory's and Chicago Creek, is now deemed almost a settled point, since the population and interests involved will demand it soon. Should the project of a railroad beyond the Range appear premature, a wagon road could be easily constructed into the Middle Park, by which the route from the Missouri to the Great Salt Lake and California would be materially shortened. Timber and good stone are plenty in all this region, while the winters, though cold, are no worse than in Northern New York or Wisconsin, even at a distance of only ten miles from perpetual snow. As to the valley of Clear Creek, it produces earlier grass and is more sheltered from winter storms than any other part of the mountain region, or even the Plains beyond the South Platte. Furthermore, a good wagon road is now used between Middle and South Parks, at an altitude of 11,000 feet above the sea, while the Pass by the head of Clear Creek would not exceed 7,800 to 8,200 feet.

## ORIGINAL BAROMETRICAL OBSERVATION OF HEIGHTS.

Golden City 5,240 feet above the level of the sea.

Table Mountain near G. C. 6,110 feet above level of sea.

North Clear Creek at mouth of Gregory's Gulch, 6,974 feet above the sea.

Main Clear Creek at Idahoe, 6,545 feet above the sea.

## INDIAN TRIBES.

The principal Indian tribes on the Platte are the Cheyennes and Arrapahoes, and on the western slope and in the Parks are situated the Utes. Besides these, wandering bands of Sioux, Kioways, Camanches and Apaches frequently visit the valley of the Platte. None of these tribes have yet displayed any hostile feelings towards the whites, but the non-extinction of the Indian title to the territory, and entire absence of any military posts have produced apprehensions that a collision might occur. We are pleased to learn that speedy attempts will be made by Government to concentrate the Cheyennes and Arrapahoes on reservations near the Arkansas River, since such a course is imperatively demanded by the peculiar circumstances of our condition.

## ADDITIONAL REMARKS.

For the information of Eastern readers unacquainted with our "peculiar institutions," the following brief articles have been collated:

*Routes to the Gold Region.*—The principal emigration, the past year, has been over the great military road from St Joseph and Leavenworth, via Marysville, the Little Blue River and Ft. Kearney, and thence by the valley of the Platte. The roads from Omaha, Nebraska City and Plattsmouth make a junction with this road near Ft. Kearney. This great highway will, we believe, remain the principal route to Denver and the adjacent mines, since it possesses superior advantages to any yet explored. The Great Salt Lake Mail Route branches from this road at Julesburgh, or Morrell's Crossing, above the junction of the North and South Platte and about 200 miles east of Denver. A large emigration has also passed over the road leading up the Arkansas, but Indian troubbles have rendered it so insecure that few have ventured to return by it. During the summer, a surveying party employed by the City of Leavenworth made a reconnoisance of a road from that place to Ft. Riley and thence by the Smoky Hill Fork of Kansas River to Colorado City and Denver. Their report that the route was direct and feasible does not appear to have induced many to attempt its passage, though it is confidently expected by those interested that next year it will be a favorite with emigrants and freighters. The various guide books published and in press, will give the emigrants of next year all necessary information in regard to the facilities and accommodations by the various routes, but we advise those intending to cross the Plains next year by private conveyance, to subscribe now to a weekly newspaper published here and keep fully advised in regard to this and all other important matters.

*Communications with the East.*—Taking into consideration the vast and almost sterile desert separating this region from Eastern Kansas and Nebraska, we may safely say that no emigrants to a new country have ever possessed such facilities of communication with their former homes as have been enjoyed by us. Last year, while yet the reports of the gold discoveries were vague, and Cherry Creek alone afforded *a prospect*, Messrs. Jones, Russell & Co., of Leavenworth, established a stage line from that city to Denver, a distance of over 600 miles, and even ran a line of daily stages over it each way. Such an enterprise, in view of the novelty and uncertainty of the discoveries made, and the wild region traversed by the coaches, has never been equalled. The daily arrival of these coaches and the confidence that there was so powerful a link yet binding them to their eastern homes, alone retained in Denver the discouraged inhabitants during the stampede of April, 1859. Over $110,000 were irrevocably sunk by the company during the year, but that sum is insignificant compared with the services rendered to the country. This spring, Messrs. J. R. & Co., disposed of their Stage and Express business to the Central Overland California and Pike's Peak Express Co., composed of wealthy Eastern and Western capitalists. This company have run a tri-weekly line of coaches between St. Joseph and Leavenworth and Denver, conveying passengers, treasure, light freight and an express mail, the time through being six days, and soon to be reduced to five. This company also run a weekly line of coaches from Julesburgh to Great Salt Lake City, carrying the U. S. Mail, and also are proprietors of the Pony Express from St. Joseph to San Francisco. A mail route having being established between Julesburgh and Denver and the contract awarded to the Western Stage Co., well known through the Western States, that company have recently established a weekly stage line between Omaha and Nebraska and will probably soon increase their service to a tri-weekly one.

The General Government having recently concluded a contract for the construction of a telegraph from the Missouri river to California, it is probable that the contractors will find it to their interest to make our Gold Region a point on their line.

The majority of the freight across the Plains has been conveyed by private trains, but a large share has been transported by private freighting companies, among which, Jones & Cartwright of Leavenworth; Alex. Majors of the same place; D. D. White & Co. of Atchison, and A. Warren & Co. and Bruce & Co. of St. Joseph, have been the most eminent. Messrs. Jones & Cartwright have made weekly trips, being 21 during the season, including 600 wagons drawn by five yoke of oxen each and carrying three tons apiece. The average time has been forty days and price of freight eight to ten cents per pound.

The Central Overland California and Pike's Peak Express

will shortly establish a fast express freight line from St. Joseph to Denver taking goods through in fourteen days. Messrs. Hinckley & Co. contemplate a similar enterprise.

*Cities and Towns.*—Brief mention only can be made of the various towns that have already sprung up in the Gold Region.

Denver, which now comprises the formerly distinct towns of Denver city, Auraria and Highland, is the principal and largest town in the new territory. Founded in the autumn of 1858 it developed rapidly the following year in spite of the panic and stampede, and during the past season has increased with a stability and rapidity novel even to those conversant with the growth of western cities.

Many fine brick edifices have been erected this summer and every trade and profession has now a representative. Denver has a population of over 6000. Golden city, twelve miles west of Denver and on Vasquez Fork or Clear Creek was laid out in June 1859, and is now the second city in the gold region. Occupying the most advantageous position to the Quartz Mines, with excellent water power and surrounded by a fine agricultural country, it must become a populous and important town.

Boulder City, on Boulder Creek, at its outlet from the mountains, possesses a fine site and a rich farming district to support it.

Golden Gate, Mt. Vernon and Bradford are all located at the base of the mountains and present peculiar advantages to those in quest of a romantic or picturesque residence.

Colorado City, six miles from the base of Pike's Peak is surrounded by magnificent scenery and objects of interest to the tourist. It already possesses a fair trade and is the largest of the southern towns.

Fountain City, occupies the old site of Pueblo on the Arkansas at the mouth of the Fontaine qui bouille, and on the route to Santa Fe.

The mining towns are numerous and have sprung up rapidly wherever "the color" has been found. Mountain City, Central City, Nevada and Missouri City, all situated in the great Quartz Region, if consolidated would represent a city of several thousand inhabitants. They all contain many fine edifices in addition to the Quartz Mills. A reference to the Table will give a fair idea of their relative importance.

Idahoe on South Clear Creek is a flourishing village and will next year become a place of first importance.

Tarryall, at the head of the Platte, Breckenridge at the head of the Blue, and Canon City in California Gulch, are all towns of local importance and increasing rapidly.

# BOTANICAL.

The Flora of Western Kansas and of the Rocky Mountain chain presents many striking and curious features. After passing Ft. Kearney upon the Platte, we notice several new forms and a totally different appearance of the genera prevalent, constituting the vegetation of the Plains. The vast ascending plain which extends from the Missouri river to the Mountains and which has rapidly risen from 740 feet altitude at Ft. Leavenworth to 2500 feet at Ft. Kearney, becomes more and more arid and sandy: the only deciduous trees we find after leaving the head of the Little Blue and cross the dividing ridge between that stream and the Platte are *Negundo aceroides* (box alder) *Populus angulata* (cottonwood,) *Salix conifera* (willow) *S. tristis*, Cornus sericea (dogwood,) *Fraxinus juglandifolia* (ash). After however passing the upper crossing of the Platte River, we rarely see any trees of any kind whatever until we reach the vicinity of Beaver Creek, where a few gnarled cottonwoods occur; these increase in frequency and number until we reach the vicinity of Fort St. Vrain, from which point the South Platte is generally fringed with a new species or rather a different kind of cottonwood approaching *Populus levigata*. The numerous branches of the South Platte, which have their origin in the mountains are also sparsely fringed with cottonwood, willow, dogwood, cherry, currant and gooseberry bushes. When, however we enter the mountains, we begin to find that the banks of Vasquez Fork (Clear Creek), Bear, Ralston's and Boulder Creeks and St. Vrain River and the neighboring mountains are covered with noble forests of Pines and Firs and the streams fringed with various deciduous trees and shrubs, such as *Populus Levigata Populus tremuloides* (aspen,) *Betula glandulosa* (Birch,) *Almus glanca* (Alder,) *Acer tripartitum* (Maple,) *Cerasus serotina* (Choke Cherry,) *Salix conifera* (Willow) *Aronia alnifolia*, and an innumerable variety of Gooseberry, Currant and Raspberry bushes.

In the vast Plains of the Arkansas and Platte Rivers, and the Republican and Smoky Hill Forks of the Kansas River, the prevailing plants are *Cactaceae, Graminae, Leguminosae,* and *Compositae*, with a few *Labiatae* and *Liliaceae* intermixed; this proportion seems to hold good till we reach the foothills of the Rocky Mountain range; here we find a greater variety of Species, as well as of Genera and Classes. The *Gramineae* seem to diminish in number, but the *Cruciferae*, rare in the prairies and Eastern Kansas, become prodigously increased, while the *Compositae*, reduced in number, are replaced by *Leguminosae, Ranunculacea* and *Geraniae* with numerous gay and brilliant *Labiatae*. Indeed some of our mountain meadows will outvie any Eastern garden by the extraordinary brilliancy and profusion of its Alpine flowers, which in this pure and rare atmosphere seems to imbibe some the intensest rays of the sun. The climatic condition of the country seems incongruous with such a floral profusion; for nine months in the year overshadowed by the Snowy Range and watered by streams whose origin is in perpetual snows, yet upon the 21st of April 1860, the hill-sides were clothed with numerous flowers and green with grasses; *Cactaceae* (species Mamillaria) covering hill tops at an altitude of 5800 feet above the sea with red rosettes of flowers. Yet at this same period in the prairies eastward all vegetation was dry and dead and as yet unquickened by the heat of the sun.

As to the capabilities of the country at the foot of the mountains for agricultural purposes, a great diversity of opinion exists even among the oldest setlers, but as this year (1860) is the first one in which any general and extensive attempts have yet been made to develop the capacity of the soil, it is difficult to form a correct opinion on the subject. Last year is represented as having been quite dry and but little rain fell this year until June 18th, since which there has been abundance. So important a branch of industry requires time for a final decision and a favorable one is so necessary in a region cut off entirely from agricultural districts, we believe that attempts will not be readily abandoned. There is a good area of arable and fertile soil, but the dryness early in the spring and violent winds retard so much the growth of the cereals that we cannot yet anticipate a home supply. Irrigation in favorable localities will remedy the inconveniences of drouth, yet so short is the season, free from frosts, that the cultivation of fruit trees, Indian corn and more tender cereals will be very limited.

*Climate.*—It may not be amiss, here to state, that no just decision in regard to the climate can yet be made. Last year, as already stated, was very dry, and a similar condition was predicted for this year, and with fulfillment up to the middle of June, since when, there has been a copious shower nearly every afternoon in the Mountains and extending to the Platte. "One swallow does not make a summer," nor the experience of a single year decide the meteorology of a a country. The showers mentioned all originate in the Snowy Range, are accompanied by thunder and lightning, and generally commence from 2 to 4 o'clock P. M., continuing from ten minutes to two hours. During the preceding dry season, the atmosphere appeared to be in a peculiar electrical state, producing various phenomena, such as affecting seriously the megnetic needle, &c. Thus far, the climate has proved to be very healthy, and though the extreme rarity of the atmosphere produces relaxation and lassitude, the great heat of the sun amounting several times to 103° to 106° in the shade, appears to produce no inconvenience.

## CATALOGUE OF PLANTS OBSERVED AND BOTANICAL REGISTER KEPT AT GOLDEN CITY, APRIL, 21st., TO JULY 21st., 1860.

Altitude of places of observation from 5,240 to 5800 feet above the level of the sea. Longitude, 105°18′ W. of Greenwich—Latitude, 39°40′ N.

### APRIL, 21st.

Delphinum exaltatum
" paucifloram (?)
Agrostis polymorpha "
Claytonia virginica.
Cactus opuntia.
Ribes aureum.

Senicio aurea.
Euchroma coccinea.
Mamillaria—sp. und *
Baptisia—sp. und.
Carex wildenvii.
Viola linguae folia.

### APRIL, 27th.

Astragalus goniatus.
" missouriensis.
Pinns resmosa. or variabilis.

Enothera pygmaea.
Berheris aqui folia.

### MAY, 2d.

Almus glanca.
Populus tremuloides.
" levigata.
Troximon cuspidaturn.

Corydalis scoulati.
Cerasus serotina
Viola canadensis.
" pedàta.

* Species undetermined.

## MAY, 6th.

Aronia alnifolia.
Acer tripartitum.
Allium tricocum.
Anemone pateus.
Fragaria virginiana.
Ribes sanguineum.
Achillea tomentosa.
Camelnia barbaraefolia.
Cerastium Vulgatum.

Nasturtium tanacetifolium.
Potentilla pulcherrima.
Xerophyllum asphodeloides.
Myosotis stricta.
Astragalus purshii.
Ranunculus abortrivus,
Stanleya integrifolia
Purshia tridentata,
Pisum—sp. und.

## MAY, 20th.

Scutillaria parbula.
Sida coccinea.
Spergula rubra.
Pinus variabilis.
Convallaria racemosa.
Delphinum viresceus.

Eulophus triternatus.
Henchera tracteata.
Geranium dissectum.
Rubus epectabilis.
Cardamine—sp. und.

## JUNE, 10th.

Argemono mexicana.
Lupinus perenis.
Vicia americana.
Arabis paleata.
Hydrophyllum canadensis.

Astragalus canadensis.
Echino spernum lappula.
Salix conifera.
Quncus tennis.
L. polyphyllus.

## JUNE, 23d.

Pinus fraseri.
Gaura biennis.
Oxytropis lamberti.
Potentilla argentea.
Aquilegia cerulea.

Betula glandulosa.
Enothera biennis (?)
Leoutidon taraxacum.
Festuca—sp. und.
Helianthus rigidus.

## JULY, 6th.

Dodecatheon medea.
Mentha viridis.

Astragalus minuta.
Juniperus virginiana.

Galium boréale.
Elymus hirsuta.
Yucca plamentosa.
Mimulus luteus.
Chiropodium vulgare.
Epilobium alpinum.
Epilobium coloratum.
Clematis virginiana.
Anemone virginiana.

Corallorhiza multiflora.
Calochertus luteus.
Sorbus—sp. und.
Cynoglossum virginiana.
Monarda didyma.
Munulus luteus(?)
Asclipias—sp. und.
Cynoglossum amplexicaule.

JULY, 20th.

Esquisetum hyemale.
Ranunculus limosus.
Chiropodium album.
Poa serotina.
Astragaliss, nov. species.
Apocynum androsemifolium.
Petalostemon violaceum.
Sesleria dactyloides.

Euphorbia marginata.
Asclipias cornuti.
Blitum capitatum.
Androsace—sp. und.
Physallis viscosa.
Baptisia cerulea.
Draba—sp. und.

# NATURAL HISTORY.

The fauna of the region discussed, does not include a number of the classes, and in those represented is not remarkably fertile in genera and species. We give a simple statement of the animals noticed by ourselves, or well known to exist within the limits of the mining region.

## MAMMALIA.

CARNIVORA.
Canis latraus, *coyote.*
" velox, *kit fox.*
" nubiliss, *dusky wolf.*
" americannus, *wolf.*
" lycaon
" argentatus, *silver wolf.*
Ursus horribilis, *grizzly bear.*
" *species und.*
Lutra americana, *otter.*
Gulo, *sp. und*, *wolverine.*
Felis montana, *wild cat.*
Felis cougar, *panther.*

RODENTIA.
Arctomys ludoviciana *p. dog.*

Capra americana, *mountain goat.*
Ovis montana, *mountain sheep.*
Cervus alces, *elk.*
" macrotis, *black-tailed deer.*
Cervus alces, virginiana, *deer.*
Bison americanus, *buffalo.*

AVES.
Corvus corone, *crow.*
" corax, *raven.*
" cristatus, *blue-jay.*
" stelleri, *jay.*
" pica, *magpie.*

| | | | |
|---|---|---|---|
| Putorius vison, | *mink.* | Tetraeurophasianus, | *pheas-ant.* |
| Tamias striatus | *ground squirrel.* | | |
| Mus, *sp. und.* | *mouse.* | Troglodytes fulvos, | *wren.* |
| Sciurus, *sp. und.* | *squirrel.* | Emberiza pecoris, | *bunting.* |
| Mustela martes, | *pine martin.* | Alcedo alcyon, | *kingfisher.* |
| Mephitis americana, | *skunk.* | Hirundo, *sp. und.* | *swallow.* |
| Castor americannus, | *beaver.* | Anas, *sp. und.* | *duck.* |
| Ruminantia. | | Charadrius vociferous, | *killdeer.* |
| Antilocapra americana, | *antelope.* | Anser canadiensis, | *goose.* |
| | | Ardea, *sp. und.* | *heron.* |

## REPTILIA.

Among the animals of this class, the following appear to be peculiar. *Agamia cornuti*, or horned frog—*Crotalus* species undetermined, rattlesnake. *Entamia sirtalis*,(?) garter snake. Also in Spring Gulch, (Clear Creek Mining Region) a lacertian, having the head of a frog, four toes on each foot, no branchiae—body spotted brown, yellow and green, tail flat, no apparent scales on body—size about seven inches.

We have not seen nor heard of any fish in abundance except the speckled trout, (a new variety.)

The entomology of the country, under consideration, is fertile, including many new varieties, especially of *cicadæ*, *grylli* and kindred insects. We are pleased to learn, that a collection of the rare and new species is being made at Denver, which will materially assist in systematizing this branch of our Natural History.

# GEOLOGICAL.

The science of Geology, which within the past fifty years, has risen from a mere skeleton of hypotheses to the dignity of an exact science, has received during that time from American research and talent, an impulse and elucidation that have materially aided its development. The magnificent series of geological surveys made by the State governments, have not been excelled in utility of purpose, or magnificence of results, both scientific and politico-economical. The territory, however, between the Missouri River and the Pacific, has as yet, been neglected, or only casually examined. The great Mountain Range, which comprises a portion of those extraordinary Cordilleras, extending from the Arctic circle on the north, to the Straits of Magellan on the south, comprise in itself, a study full of interest and instruction. The South American portion of the chain, known as the Andes, have been thoroughly examined, with results full of importance to science, and it is to be hoped that the Rocky Mountains also will soon receive that careful research and treatment which they demand from the practical Geologist.

The country for four hundred miles to the east, is underlaid by rocks of the secondary formation, mostly of the cretaceous groups. But few outcrops occur, the whole formation appearing to occupy its primitive position undisturbed, and thus but few opportunities are afforded of examining the exact relation of the strata. The superincumbent soil would indicate a predominance of siliceous rocks, though outcrops of chalk have been noticed on the Republican Fork. Again, the absence of outcrops and escarpments and also of artificial sections (obtainable from mines and extensive excavations) have prevented an inspection of the paleontological character of the strata. Reaching the mountains, passing over the tertiary formation at their base, we find a portion of the exterior ranges and parallel ridges composed of sandstone metamorphic, and, while retaining their planes of stratification, present strongly defined planes of cleavage and foliation. As we progress towards the axial or Snowy Range, we find the various ranks of mountain elevations, composed of plutonic rocks, though with marked differences as to structure and mineralogical character; until arriving at the great snow-capped axis, the bold precipices and disrupted fragments of solid granite, proclaim the acme of igneous action. The mining region, situated between the axial and exterior ranges, is composed of talcose, porphyritic, schorly, and ordinary granite and syenite, and thence to the outer lines, the formation becomes less massive and homogenous, and assumes gradually a schistose and gneissoid character. There is no doubt but that a large proportion of the lower fossiliferious strata are represented, but metamorphic action has been so marked as to destroy the distinctive character, and produce a general uniformity of structure. The whole mountain belt occupies an average breadth of about 75 miles, the various ranges being parallel to the axis, though cut through by frequent cross valleys, which convey to the Plains below, the hundred water courses originating in the snowy reservoirs. The auriferous quartz viens have thus far been discovered in a belt 20 miles wide, and immediately east of the Snowy Range, though it is highly probable that similar veins occur on the western slope. The quartz veins found in the granite east of the above mentioned belt, as examined on the surface, are usually of the milky or snowy character, closely crystalline and devoid of pyrites and gold. It may be remarked, of all the mountain formations, that their durability diminishes as we pass eastward from the main range, until reaching the outer ranges, we find them all undergoing a rapid and destructive disintegration. The Plains for several miles from the base, are covered with fragments of the disrupted rocks, and, as we proceed yet further eastward, the debris becomes more and more comminuted till it forms those extensive depositions of micaceous sand that occupy the whole valley of the Platte, while the liberated felspar forms those alkaline encrustations that cover the surface of the same region with a snowy deposite. Similar phenomena occur on all the other rivers heading in the Mountains, and we may find a solution to many of the peculiar aspects of the so-called "Great American Desert," in the gradual decomposition of the Rocky Mountains and the transportation of the debris over a vast territory, and which by recomposition have conferred peculiar mineralogical aspects on the tertiary formations where found.

Immediately east of the mountains we find a broad tertiary basin, displaying outcrops of sandstone and conglomerate, evidently formed of disintegrated granite, united by a siliceous cement, with layers of siliceous limestone, all conformable in dip and strike with the axial mountain range. Above these and inconformably, is a layer of brown coal, (see Mineralogy) interstratified with butuminous shales and overlaid by a thick stratum of white sandstone or grit. This tertiary basin is traceable north and south and parallel with the mountains for a distance of 80 miles, and has an average height of 5000 feet above the sea.

The only trappean or volcanic rocks yet noticed by the writers are confined to two peculiar table mountains, near Golden City, and on either side of Vasquez Fork. These two elevations, once united and forming one, are now separated by the stream, which has gradually worn its channel down to a depth of 590 feet below their summits, and are a mile distant from the mountain range proper. Each mountain is about eight miles in circumference, of irregular outline, and with level summits, bordered by a perpendicular precipice, from 50 to 180 feet high, of columner basalt and amygoaloid; from the foot of this precipice they slope at an angle of 45°, the slope being composed of fallen fragments of basalt. This basalt rests immediately on a late tertiary sandstone and presents the appearance of two distinct eruptions, and of subaqueous formation. Silicified wood is found in large quantities, sometimes including the complete trunks of trees transformed to compact stone, and all of them in the vicinity of basalt. We know of no other volcanic rocks this side of the mountains, though they may exist.

To return to the mining region proper, we find all the auriferous quartz veins, situated in a great basin or depression in the mountains, and surrounded on all sides by higher elevations. Within this basin, are found the sources of Clear and the Boulder Creeks and their tributaries, and all the evidence confirms the conclusion that it is a basin of erosion. This denudation has revealed the gold bearing lodes, and by their gradual decomposition bestowed on the alluvium of the gulches and bars its coveted treasures.

An interesting question arises as to the geological age of the Rocky Mountains, and which cannot be fully decided until a thorough examination of both flanks has been made. We believe them to be of different and long separated ages; that while the central ranges were protruded subsequent to a portion of the secondary groups, and anterior to the tertiary, the exterior eastern ranges were elevated subsequent to a portion of the tertiary; that the whole have been subjected to frequent, long continued, and often violent disturbances both of elevation and depression, and under the influence of strong aqueous action. Such a hypothesis would represent the highest Mountain Range of the United States as the youngest also.

Such is a brief and imperfect sketch of the Geological features of this interesting region, and we would earnestly repeat our hope that the interest now converging to its rich mineral resources, will induce some of our eminent practical Geologists to visit the country and give it a thorough and systematic survey. Such a labor is demanded, and would be appreciated both in its purely scientific and its economical aspects.*

* The writers intend, should opportunity and leisure offer, to make during the autumn, a more thorough examination of the Geology of the mountains and adjacent country.

# MINERALOGICAL.

As in all plutonic mountain ranges, we find the country under discussion, peculiarly rich and varied in its minerals. The granitic character of the rocks gives a predominance to their constituents, and we find quartz, felspar, mica, tourmaline, garnet and albite abundantly disseminated throughout the whole area. The quartzose and felspathic are especially numerous and interesting, and nearly all the classified minerals containing those primaries in excess are to be found abundant. Quartz, colorless, white, green, yellow and blue, imitative in its hues of all the gems, is found widely dispersed. Pure felspar, both white and flesh-colored, is frequent. Black and transparent mica are found in plates of considerable size. The decomposition of the falspathic rocks have produced occasional deposites of kaolin very pure and free from metalic admixtures. Talc, both in situ intercalated with granite, and deposited by subsidence from aqueous erosion, is found in abundance. Decided magnesian minerals except talc and hornblende, has not yet been found, though their presence might be predicted on the geological structure of the country. Hornblende appears in the metamorphic rocks. Sulphate of lime, in the form of fibrous and crystalline selenite and alabaster, is frequent and beautiful cabinet specimens may be obtained. Carbonate of lime in the form of sileceous limestone is found east of the mountains, and some sufficiently pure for the manufacture of lime. Crystallized carbonate of lime in the form of calc-spar is also found. Coal is also found in the valley, (see Geology) beneath a white granular sandstone and in veins, interstratified with shale, of from one to thirty inches thick. It is apparently of the tertiary formations, though no distinct fossils have been found to decide the matter paleontologically,* yet the general character of the coal itself, the contiguous rocks and plausible theory of a geological modern formation of the whole country, would provoke the decision that this is one of the most recent carbonaceous deposites on the continent. The coal obtained at depths below atmospheric influences, is compact, breaks with a slight-conchoidal fracture, glossy and clean. We have had no opportunity as yet to test specific gravity or analyze the coal. It is mined, and used extensively by blacksmiths throughout the country and appears to contain more bitumnious and volatile matter than any fuel we ever saw; as the smiths say, it is very *resinous*. It would be a valuable article for the manufacture of coal oil. There appears to be an abundance of it, and several pits have been opened in the outcrops.

Native alum in crystalline masses has been found in the valley, and is mostly a pure sulphate of alumina and potassa, though some specimens show a tendency to substitution of iron for potassa. The following metals have been found native and mostly in immediate juxtaposition, gold (see next article) iron in the gulches with gold attached; silver in small particles; copper in scales attached to auriferous quartz. Several parties who have obtained impure gold from their

---

\* In the carboniferous sandstone a few miles north of Golden City, we have discovered a fossil plant, apparently a *dicotyledon*, which would indicate a tertiary formation; but the fossil was too indistinct to decide the question by a single specimen.

retorts have been disposed to call the foreign element, *platinum*. The geology of the country would indicate the presence of platinum, but we have been unable yet to discover it and from the fact that it does not amalgamate with murcury, we presume the alloy is produced by other metals. The most abundant class of the ores are the sulphurets, and thus far these have been discovered in the quartz veins, mingled with the native metals above mentioned. All the auriferous quartz contains sulphuret of iron, or iron pyrites, and in most cases in large quantities; these pyrites are found disseminated through the mass in small crystals, and frequently with large crystals associated with other sulphurets. The sulphuret of lead or galena occurs in several lodes, some of them auriferous; this galena is all argentiferous, and we have analysed specimens containing one quarter of one per cent of silver to the ton of ore, and we have no doubt but some small veins might be found richer. Copper pyrites are found in conjunction with iron pyrites and gold, but not in such quantities as to be of commercial value. Arsenical pyrites are also discovered in similar position. Blende or sulphuret of zinc is largely associated with some of the galena veins and renders their reduction and separation difficult. Sulphuret of antimony has also been noticed in the same veins. Frequent reports that cinnabar has been found in the mountains, have been heralded in the papers, sometimes endorsed by so-called mineralogists, but we have yet been unable to obtain any specimens, and would entirely discredit the reports, on the independent ground that the geology of the rocks precludes the discovery of ores of mercury.

Considerable excitement has been occasioned by the discovery of extensive metallic veins near the sources of the Blue River, and which are represented as being rich in silver. These lodes are found in porphyritic granite, and one of them the *Quandery Lode*, presents a horizontal surface of over 100 feet, produced most probably by a deflection of the vein.

Very extravagant reports have been circulated in regard to these veins, and assays have been published, representing the ore as equal if not superior to that of the celebrated Washoe Mines. The authors of this work have made several analyses resulting in $75 to $210 worth of silver to the ton of ore, but are unable to determine wether the specimens were fair representatives of the entire vein. The ore examined, consisted of sulphurets of lead and antimony, sulphuret of silver and traces of iron and perhaps gold, the residuum being the rocky matrix. This ore would be valuable in a region, where cheap labor, machinery and fuel were attainable, and where the associated metals could be readily disposed of. The discovery of similar ore is reported from the head of Fall River and other localities.

The Blue Carbonate of Copper also occurs in connection with copper pyrites, and beautiful crystalline specimens may be obtained; the green carbonate is found but not plentifully. Of the metallic oxides, that of iron is the only one found in any abundance. Magnetic iron sand is found in the gulches in connection with native gold, and is the *black sand\** usually collected with gold in the process of washing. Magnetic iron ore in their seams has also been noticed, but as it is all probably the result of decomposed pyrites, will be found to contain too much sulphur to be of commercial value. Hand specimens of specular iron ore have been brought from the foot of the Snowy Range. A few specimens of sesquioxide of iron have been noticed, and in the valley east of the Range, hydrated peroxide intercalated with ocherous clays have been found in veins, but as yet very lean and impure as an ore. It is a matter of great public concern that this valuable ore should be found in large quantities; we have the coal and limestone flux in abundance, and with plenty of good ore could soon reduce the price of castings from 20 cents per pound to a

---

\* This black sand sometimes contains tourmaline.

more reasonable price. Peroxide of manganese occurs in small quantities. Mineral waters have been found at Soda Springs near Soda Creek, a tributary of South Clear Creek, and, though no analysis has been made, appear to contain sulphate of soda, iron and a little free sulphuric acid—there are three springs within a distance of fifty feet, all of identical composition but with waters of the different temperatures of $36°$, $95°$ and $130°$.

In closing the subject we would repeat that the mineralogy of the Rocky Mountains is replete with useful and valuable metals, and deserves a careful survey and analysis. Upon the mineral wealth of the mining region, the whole future settlement and prosperity of the country depends, and it surely demands from the General Government an immediate scientific examination not only upon temporary grounds, but upon the broader ones connected with the permanent occupancy and improvement of the country. Every one must see that apart from general considerations, the establishment of a central State at the base of these mountains is a matter of great national policy. Such a State would form a strong link between the Pacific and Eastern States, and occupy an important position in the national relations to Utah and the interior Indian tribes, while its central location on the route of the great Pacific Railroad, would relieve that magnificent project from the objection that it would have no internal resources of revenue, but be dependant entirely on its termini.

# GOLD MINING IN THE ROCKY MOUNTAINS.

We do not intend in this article to write a treatise upon the inmportant subject involved, or exhaust its individual relations to our own mining region; either theme would require larger scope than our brief pamphlet affords us. But no new mining country ever discovered, demanded from friends and foes so fair and complete an exposition and well considered verdict as our own. Those who have had faith and interest in its development have provoked incredulous criticism by the exaggerated and unfounded reports they have uttered; while skeptical or deceived persons, have with equal injustice stamped the whole tale of gold as a baseless falsehood and humbug. Thus injudicious friends and self-imposed victims have combined to produce an effect, an indifferent incredulity in the minds of the public at large, in regard to the resources or prospects of our mountain country. We have hopes that the publication of our little work, though suddenly projected and inadequately executed may tend and assist to a fairer estimate than generally obtains.

We can here advert only to the bar and gulch diggings, for though they have produced nearly all the gold extracted up to date, they have proved not to be as rich as similar depósites elsewhere and in the older districts are already nearly exhausted unless worked over a second time with improved machinery. It is in the extraordinary and extensive lodes of auriferous quartz that we must seek that large and permanent supply of gold, the production of which alone will ensure the future of our new country. We have made brief notice of these veins in our Geological and Mineralogical articles, and would here repeat that the veins occur in granite, have a general direction of 15° N. E. and lie in a vertical plane, or slightly inclined therefrom. All the veins contain iron pyrites, which by decomposition near the surface, have discolored the rock to a red hue whence its term "blossom rock." Thus the veins are easily traced, even by the inexperienced. It is the very large proportion of iron pyrites (and also of other sulphurets) that has conferred upon the auriferous quartz of this country its very peculiar and distinctive qualities. In the quartz of California, most of the iron is oxidized and does not appear in large quantities. The quartz of the Carolinas and Georgia, though occupying a different geological position, contains also a large amount of pyrites, but they do not appear to have become so subject to decomposition near the surface as here. The geology of the gold region of the Ural Mountains is said to resemble that of the Rocky Mountains very much, but we are not aware of the relative amount of sulphurets. The decomposition of the pyrites has produced a peculiar structure in the quartz, coloring it red as before stated and making it cellular and of a spongy texture in many instances, as the miners call it "*burnt*," wrongly supposing its peculiar appearance due to igneous action. This cellular quartz is easily crushed and, where containing gold to any amount, is the most profitable kind to work, as the decomposition of the pyrites has released the gold and prevents loss of mercury. As we penetrate into the veins and get below the action of atmospheric influences, we find the signs of decomposition diminished and the pyrites appear in crystals of various sizes, but the quantity of gold in the quartz also increases. The very interesting problem is therefore presented of how the oxidation of the sulphurets is to be secured thoroughly and rapidly, since, unless this is solved, the old method of mining and exposing quartz to atmospheric influences before grinding or amalgamating must be resorted to, and that is a slow, tedious and *old-fogy* process.

The sulphurets of lead, copper, silver, zinc, antimony and arsenic are also detected in the same veins. The lodes have an average width of fifteen inches, though varying from five to forty inches and in the same lode never constant. Nearly every elevation in the mining district contains several lodes, frequently of unequal composition and richness. Thus far, but little attention appears to be paid to the relative value of quartz from different lodes; all appear to find a market on equal terms. Lodes are opened every week, and the extracted quartz though almost destitute of gold, is ground up at the mills, and the resulting disappointment attributed to any cause but the true one. It may be stated as a general rule, *that not one metalic vein in ten is profitable to work*, and also that it is not good business economy to rate all qualities of the same commodity at one fixed price. The estimate of the value of a vein by surface prospecting is entirely empirical and liable to great error as the subjacent quartz may produce very different results. In most of the quartz the gold exists in such finely comminuted state as to be invisible, though some specimens contain visible particles. The quartz is extracted by means of shafts and drifts and it is in the falsely economical method in which the mining is performed that a great deal of the disappointment, so far experienced, has originated. Very few shafts have been sunk below 30 to 40 feet from the surface, and any one acquainted with the nature of mineral veins will perceive the short sightedness of such a superficial course. As metallic veins are almost invariably richest at the lower points of deposition, the shafts should be sunk as far as practicable before mining is commenced; the most profitable quartz is thus obtained at the outset to the exclusion of the poorer kinds. We believe that scientific mining in these mountains will yet produce results unequalled in the history of gold, but we are desirous of reaching these results without passing through the ordeal of discouragement and failure. The owners of quartz mills should refuse to purchase or grind this mere superficial scratching, and demand a method of mining commensurate with their own expensive and superior machinery. The rock after extraction is generally piled up indifferently in one heap and thus sent to the mills; instead of which negligent course, the poorer portions, the wall rock and the metallic ores should be carefully rejected; the cost of hauling, crushing and otherwise manipulating a worthless article is thus avoided, besides one source of loss of mercury is escaped. The methods of transporting the mineral to the mills are thus far very crude and expensive, and it would well repay the owners of good lodes to obtain adequate machinery for hoisting material from their shafts and transporting quartz to the valleys.

The large amount of machinery thus far erected is of very fair quality, and considering the difficulties of transporting it over the plains, and the poor facilities for erection in the mines, we have no desire to criticise. Mills from the machine works of a score of Eastern makers are now at work, or preparing so to do, and this season will decide the standard style for future use. An examination of the annexed directory will give a clear idea of the various machines and names of makers. The general methods of amalgamation are also noticed except in case of several patent machines yet untried. We may state in general terms that the crushing or grinding machinery should be of such power and character as will reduce the quartz to an impalpable powder, as the gold is in such fine state as to require complete pulverization before it is liberated. The feeding of the mill should be uniform, as an excess or deficiency of material in the battery boxes is disadvantageous. The amalgamating machinery should be so constructed as to retain the pulverized material as long as possible in contact with the mercury. The use of amalgamated copper-plate is becoming very prevalent, and it serves the purpose of extending the mercury over a much larger amalgamating surface than can otherwise be done. A considerable loss of gold and mercury occurs through the use of pyritous quartz, and where this is excessive, the quartz should be previously roasted in contact with steam which reduces the sulphurets to sulphates, in which state they are innoxious. The exposure of tailings from pyritous quartz to atmospheric influences for some time, and then re-grinding will serve the same purpose. This oxidation of the sulphurets is a matter of deep concern to mill-owners, and in this region where pyrites are so largely associated with the gold, should receive their earnest consideration.

Too much attention cannot be paid to securing a perfect purity of mercury. We are sorry to say that a proportion of the mercury brought to this region is impure and adulterated; and a very small portion of foreign metals impairs its fluidity and prevents amalgamation with the gold, while it is difficult for the inexperienced to detect the cause. Whenever new mercury is purchased it should before using be purified by distillation with clean iron turnings or by any of the recognized chemical processes, and during use should be frequently examined, and if necessary purified. The presence of foreign metals with the gold in such large quantities, as is the case in quartz from most of the lodes, will occasion loss and much embarrassment in amalgamating, and is in our opinion one of the most formidable difficulties the mill-owner will have to contend with. Negligent or careless lubrication of the stamp or cam rods frequently introduces oil or other greasy matter into the mercury, and in such case hot water, with strong alkali dissolved in it, should be allowed to pass through the amalgamators. We would recommend as a lubricator for the stamps, tallow, with a large admixture of plumbago or black lead. Amalgamation is at all times assisted by the application of heat, and will be especially necessary in the winter. This can be done by actual application to the amalgamator within the limits of 800° Farenheit. Where this is not practicable the water can be heated either directly or by means of the waste steam, which can be done in various ways that may be suggested, care being taken that no injurious substances are introduced into the water in the process. The retorts used in distillation, the mercury vessels and buckskin amalgam bags, should be kept clean and occasionally washed in strong alkaline water. The amalgam remaining after squeezing through a thick, tight buckskin bag, should contain one part of mercury and two parts of gold (latter inclusive of alloyed metals). The mercury that passes through the bag contains some gold in proportions relative to the texture of the bag. Distillation should be conducted at a heat but little above the evaporating point of mercury (662° Farenheit), since several other metals are volatile at a higher heat, and should be continued till all the mercury has passed over.

As the auriferous lodes all contain other metals, some of which are collected with the gold, we will find the latter of variable value according to the amount of this accidental alloy. Since all gold is received at certain fixed rates, irrespective of quality within certain limits, it behooves the mill-owner, who exercises care and science in his operations, to obtain the full value of his gold without reference to these arbitrary rates, which place him on a level with his careless and perchance dishonest neighbor. With this view, his gold should be from time to time melted in quantity and cast into homogenous bars or ingots, which should be analyzed or assayed by competent parties and their value stamped upon them.

The following special remarks have been added since the body of the work has been prepared as presenting in a succinct manner matters of direct importance to the gold miner.

*Prospecting.*—It has hitherto been usual for prospecters to determine the value of a lode by the following method: A certain weight or quantity of the quartz and associated dirt from near the surface is pulverized in a mortar, and the gold is carefully separated by means of mercury and washing, and the proportion thus obtained is assumed as that of the entire lode. This method is very erroneous, and has been the occasion of much disappointment and loss of labor and money. It should be recollected that as the mountains themselves were once much more elevated, so the veins extended upwards. The action of the elements has gradually eroded even the solid rocks, and while most of the debris has been transported to the valleys, much of the gold and heavier material remains *in situ*, and thus the prospecter obtains from the surface diggings, the result of Nature's quiet quartz mill operating for years. The wise mill owner will never put his entire trust in pay-dirt and surface prospects. Dig to the solid rock!

*Ownership of Lodes.*—Mill owners should own or control sufficient quartz to run their mills; in other words should be entirely independent of other parties in their supply of quartz. Thus only can the mill owner secure a constant and full supply of material free from wall rock and other worthless matter, while a concentration of all the operations in one management will so economise the general processes, that even the leaner qualities of quartz can be worked with success.

*Mining Machinery.*—No extensive mining project can be advantageously prosecuted without the aid of machinery. Shafts after reaching a certain depth become flooded with water, requiring pumps, while the greater elevation that the material has to be raised requires cheaper and more reliable power than the ordinary windlass. As a motor the Ericsson

Caloric Engine, especially on the mountains, claims a decided preference, as being independent of the use of water, requiring but little fuel, incapable of explosion and simple in superintendence. They are already extensively used in California for mining purposes and will no doubt be extensively used here.

We must refer those interested to the approved works on mining, and to practical mechanics for detailed descriptions of the various machines and inventions used, and can only briefly mention a few of the most reliable. For pumping water from mines, the best machine is the ordinary lift pump, as it is more simple and less liable to derangement than any other, while its only objection here is the weight of pipe required, but this may be obviated where the lift is stationary by using heavy rubber-hose of the required size for all that part above the piston chamber. It may be well to say that by lift-pump we would designate a tube of equal bore from top to bottom of the shaft, having at the lower end a piston chamber bored and fitted to the piston; the stroke being from one to three feet, and the piston-rod passing up through the entire pipe. The piston-rod may be of wood suitably spliced, and its weight balanced by the use of a counter weighted rock lever. This kind of pump has never been superceded in the Cornish mines.

Many people through ignorance imagine that water can be raised here by suction as high as in the Eastern States; *i. e.*, 28 to 30 feet; forgetting that the diminished weight of the atmosphere consequent on greater elevation will not support so high a column of water. From 22 to 23 feet is the greatest height to which water can be raised anywhere in the mining region. For hoisting we prefer the friction machine with a strong brake as used in Eastern coal and iron mines, as being the safest and easiest controlled machine yet invented.

For injecting fresh air for ventilating purposes, the ordinary fan blower with canvass tube requires the least power, and is quite as efficacious as any other, especially as it is not probable that such great depths will ever be reached in the quartz mines as to require the more expensive machines.

*Oxidation of the Sulphurets.*—Particular attention has already been directed to the large quantity of sulphurets, in especial that of iron, contained in the auriferous quartz and of their injurious action. Where the richness of the quartz will not justify their oxidation artificially, it is proposed to secure this result by exposure to the elements. Such a course has been adopted for the last twenty years in the Georgia and other mines, and several crops of the precious metal thus obtained from the same rock.

*Purification of Mercury.*—Nine-tenths of the mercury brought to this region is impure, and also since the pure mercury is soon contaminated in the process of amalgamation, we give several methods of purifying it.

1st. By distilling it in a retort with one-half its weight of iron turnings or filings.

2d. By digesting it with nitric acid in a glass vessel.

3d. By agitating it with a solution in water of corrosive sublimate, or of sesquichloride of iron.

Either of the processes will remove all the more oxidizable metals.

*Chemistry for the Gold Miner.*—Though laboratories have been established where chemical analyses can be obtained, it may be convenient for the mill-owner to determine the value of his own gold. As the associated metal is mostly silver, the following process may be followed : Melt in a black lead crucible one part of the gold and four parts pure silver by weight; digest the alloy thus made in concentrated nitric acid, which will dissolve the silver and leave the gold in the form of a brown precipitate in powder, which must be collected and carefully weighed. The loss will represent silver. This process is called "Quartation," and is used in all the mints, being founded on the chemical principle, that when an alloy is composed of one part gold and *at least* four parts silver, all the latter metal is dissolved out by nitric acid.

Gold is soluble only in *aqua-regia* composed of one part nitric and one part muriatic acid, and can always be precipitated from any solution by the addition of a solution in water of the oxalate of ammonia or of the protosulphate of iron.

The proprietor of the mill or the local manager should exercise at all times a careful supervision over every branch of the processes, since no portion can be safely confided without reserve to ordinary employees. As many are inexperienced either in one branch or all, we submit for their guidance the following suggestions as touching upon the most important duties devolving upon him.

As most of the machinery is set up on foundations and in frame work of pine wood, which yields readily to vibration, all nuts, keys &c. should be examined from time to time and if necessary tighten up; some mills are already racked and injured from neglect in this respect. The engineer should never be allowed to carry steam beyond maximum pressure, and should be required to clean out the flues at least once a day. If the feed water be *riley*, the boiler should be frequently *blown down* to prevent burning of the flues or shell. Where great speed of piston is attained, oiling the steam cylinder with tallow should not be neglected. The manager should attend personally to the lubrication of the cam shaft and the pestle rods, so that no grease is allowed to drop into the batteries. The feeding of quartz to the batteries should be uniform, since too much chokes them and prevents full action, and too little may expose the battery bed and break it or the stamps. The quartz on its delivery at the mill should be carefully inspected and all wall rock, metallic ores, &c., rejected, and the quartz at all times kept in a clean place;

in fact the quartz from the time it is quarried till it is discharged impoverished from the tail-sluice cannot be too carefully protected from the admixture of foreign substances, which cannot but do harm in one way or another.

The mercury used in the amalgamating cannot be too frequently examined. When purchased it should be tested and purified, especially as most of the mercury brought to this country is impure or adulterated. Analysis have detected lead, tin, nickel, arsenic, zinc and many other foreign substances, and nothing but absolutely pure mercury is fit for use. It should also be carefully examined, and if necessary purified, after every retorting. The quantity used should be ascertained by weighing when introduced into the amalgamators and after retorting, so as to detect extraordinary losses and remedy them. Every mill should secure an exclusive source of pure water so as to be independent of the carelessness or criminality of others, introducing grease and other deleterious matters into it. Preparations should now be made for heating the water used in the winter season, and securing full supply free from danger of frosts. The retorting of the amalgam is a delicate process, though very rudely performed generally, and should be done under the careful inspection of the manager, who should insist upon an absolute cleanliness of the apparatus used and of the person or persons conducting the process; while care is taken that the fumes of the mercury do not escape, since they may produce salivation and other distressing symptoms.

Finally, the proprietor should fully recognise the fact, that he is engaged in an occupation involving the most delicate principles of mechanics, chemistry and metallurgy, and if not conversant with these himself, he should seek the most skillful advice and counsel of others to aid in perfecting the various processes.

Such are a few of the most salient points in a new enterprise that has already enlisted the interests of thousands and secured the investment of a large amount of capital in spite of peculiar and formidable difficulties. Most of the mills are in the hands of inexperienced persons, who have before them an occupation involving some of the nicest principles of mechanics, metallurgy and chemistry. The extraction of gold from the quartz of the Rocky Mountains is probably a more difficult and complicated matter than any other gold mining process in the world, since here in addition to the minute subdivisions of the gold and the presence of iron pyrites are several metals which destroy the vivacity of the mercury and reduce the value of the gold. The inexperienced should recollect that to them is now confided not only their own fortune, but in a degree that of the whole country, since their general disaster will seriously delay the general advance in spite of the stability and extent of our mineral resources. They should be careful to secure the most reliable and scientific information in their power and apply it with rigid adherence to detail and economy. Thus experience gradually gained without spasmodic fortune will ensure their success beyond a peradventure.

In view of the importance and extent of the quartz mining interest in this region, it seems advisable that the mill-owners should form a permanent association for the collection and examination of minerals, the collation of statistics and for meeting at stated times for an interchange of views and comparison of experience. Such an institution would amply repay its cost and sustenance, and by substituting the experience of one for the wholesale experience of all, will materially assist in the perfect and speedy development of the various processes. Such associations have proved very valuable in California and other mining countries.

# STATISTICS.

The statistics of the mills in operation and preparing to operate have been arranged in tabular form for more convenient reference and comparison. The tables contain all the mills that had reached the Clear Creek Mining Region up to the date of publication, but do not include all the mills in the Boulder District. Our blanks requesting information were distributed through the latter region at an early date, giving the owners ample time to fill them out and return, but they have in most instances failed to do so, probably on account of mishaps or failures in getting machinery into operation. In addition to the mills in the Boulder Region in the annexed tables, there are reported 4 steam mills, 5 water mills and 29 rastras.*

A summary of the details makes the number of steam mills in the Clear Creek Region 71—total number of stamps 609, of an average weight of 416 lbs., and average fall of

---

*There appears to be considerable latitude allowed in the orthography of this word, many pronouncing and spelling it as *Arastra*. There is a Spanish verb, *Rastrar*, to drag, and the substantives, *Rastra*, a sled, something dragged, and *Rastro* with same signification. There is also a verb, *Arrastrar*, to creep, to crawl, to drag, but no derivative noun. We have therefore for obvious reasons, adopted Rastra, especially as the word is so used in California.

16¼ inches. The effect of these stamps reduced to a fall of one foot in one minute is equal to 14,715,922 lbs., or 446 horse power, and adding to this for friction and auxiliary machines we have 715 horse power as the labor performed by these engines, though none are worked up to their full capacity, and many work only half their actual power.

There are 38 water mills in the same region with 230 stamps of average weight of 352 lbs. and average fall of 14¼ inches. The effect of these stamps reduced to fall of one foot in one minute is 2,869,383 lbs. or 87 horse power, and adding for friction, &c., we have 145 horse power as the index of power actually used in the water mills. There are also 50 rastras requiring about 100 horse power. The total horse power therefore in actual use in this region in grinding quartz is 960, with capacity of increase to 1300 without additional motors. We estimate the horse power in use in the Boulder region at 150.

The manufacturers of the machinery are various; but several establishments appear to have received a large number of orders. P. W. Gates & Co., Chicago, have furnished 15 steam engines and 225 stamps and fixtures. R. C. Totten & Co., St. Louis, 8 engines and 122 stamps. Gaty, McCune & Co., St. Louis, 8 engines and 72 stamps. Maison, Wilson & Co., Leavenworth, K. T., 3 engines and 53 stamps. Dowdle & Co., St. Louis, 3 engines and 38 stamps. Johnson & Emerson, Alton, Ill., 4 engines and 24 stamps. Lawrence Machine Shop, Lawrence, Mass., 5 engines.

Many patent amalgamators are in use. Among them are eleven Eureka Amalgamators and three Coleman's Amalgamators.

Some few of the mills possess peculiar machinery, which could not be included in the columns of the tables, and reference is therefore made in such cases to an appendix.

In the table of Rastras, where horizontal water wheels are

used, it is understood that as many water-wheels are used as there are rastras.

In all dates the year 1860 is understood, unless otherwise expressed.

Where owners of mills are from different States, the residence of the first party only is given.

# APPENDIX.

No. 1. The Black Hawk Mills allow the ground quartz &c. to pass from the shaking tables to an endless blanket running on rollers, by which means the heavier particles including the sulphurets are caught beneath the blanket. The material thus collected is placed in German Amalgamating Barrels consisting of iron cylinders revolving on their axes and containing heavy iron balls, which pulverize and amalgamate.

No. 2. The Ford Mining Co., and Almyr & Co., do not use stamps. The quartz is first passed through two coarse and then through two fine *McAdamizers*, by which it is reduced to small fragments; it is then passed through three coarse and two fine Ellithorpe pulverizers—the first of these consisting of conical grinding surfaces, (like a coffee-mill) and the latter of circular plates working in contact. All this machinery is of cast iron, the grinding surfaces being chilled. The amalgamators are heated artificially.

No. 3. Smith & Chaffee, pass material from their stamps through a mill, somewhat like a grist mill, only the upper stone is stationary and the lower one revolves. These stones are of granite procured in the vicinity of their mill.

No. 4. James Burt & Co., use as a motor an Ericsson Caloric Engine of 24 inch cylinder, equal to 5 horse power—the material from the stamps passing through an iron conical grinding mill. The Caloric works fully up to estimate, but the mill reqires for perfect operation seven or eight horse power.

No. 5. Wm. Greene & Co., use no stamps, but pass their material through McAdamizers and thence through iron grinding mills—have three mills capable of grinding one cord of quartz in eight to ten hours. Think the grinding surfaces do not last long enough, and in case the quartz will pay intend to replace the mills with 12 stamps. Use cast iron amalgamator of own invention.

No. 6. These mills use as a motor, Fairchild's Patent Excelsior Wheel. This is a horizontal wheel on the turbnie principle of 12 inches in diameter and 24 long, making from 900 to 1000 revolutions per minute, and appears to be a very compact and desirable motor when a large fall and supply of water can be obtained. Messrs. Simmons, K., P. & Co. are agents.

No. 7. In addition to the mills enumerated in the tables, there are as before remarked many mills in the Boulder Region, which neglected to return answers to our circular. There are also many steam mills on the road to Clear Creek Region, the number being variously estimated from ten to thirty. Concerning these no correct information could be obtained. Preparations also being made to erect water power qnartz mills on South Clear Creek and Fall River, both which localities promise to equal in richness and importance the older districts. Parties are also preparing to build Rastras on North Clear Creek, both below Russell's and above Missouri Gulches, on Russell's and Leavenworth Gulches and on South Clear Creek and Fall River. We also hear that probably Rastras will be built and operated on some of the southerly branches of Boulder Creek.

We will be enabled in our next edition or publication to give a fuller and more detailed account of the machinery, &c. and also the practical fruits of experience and observation gathered from over *two hundred* Mills and Rastras.

# RASTRAS.

| Name of Owners | From what State | Location | Commenced Operation | Kind of Water-Wheel | Diameter of Rastra, in ft. | No. of Rastras | Diameter of Tub, in ft. | No. of Crushers | Weight of C. Stones, in lbs. |
|---|---|---|---|---|---|---|---|---|---|
| Lake & Co., | Ill. | North Clear Creek | July 18, | Undershot, | 7 | 1 | 6 | 2 | 160 |
| Crookshank & Brown, | Ia. | " | Aug. 25, | Horizontal, | 14 | 6 | 7 | 2 | |
| E. B. Holmes & Co., | Min. | " | Aug. 1, | " | 14 | 4 | 7 | 2 | |
| L. H. Bunnell, | Ia. | " | " | " | 14 | 2 | 7 | 2 | 600 |
| Kenton, Webber & Co., | Ohio | " | " | " | 14 | 6 | 7 | 2 | |
| John Eagle, | Ia. | " | " | " | 14 | 3 | 7 | 2 | |
| D. B. Cleghorn, | K. T. | " | " | " | 16 | 8 | 8 | 4 | 400 |
| Sherry & Brown, | Ill. | " | Aug. 1859, | " | 14 | 1 | 7 | 2 | 400 |
| Newlin & Co., | Ia. | " | July 1, | " | 18 | 1 | 7 | 2 | 1000 |
| Teale, Warnock & Wheeler, | N. H. | " | Aug. 1, | " | 14 | 3 | 7 | 2 | 400 |
| Shapeze, Presby & Co., | Wis. | " | June 20, | " | 16 | 1 | 8 | 4 | 800 |
| A. W. Shephard, | Ia. | " | July 17, | " | 16½ | 2 | 7 | 2 | 500 |
| W. F. Ross & Co., | " | " | July 20, | " | 16 | 1 | 7 | 2 | 500 |
| W. H Lake, | N. T. | " | July 23, | " | 14 | 4 | 8 | 4 | 700 |
| Johnson & Co., | | " | " | " | 14 | 2 | 7 | 2 | 500 |
| Geo. Beach & Co., | Ia. | " | July 23, | " | 16 | 1 | 7 | 2 | 500 |
| Ripley & Poindexter, | " | " | July 25, | " | 14 | 1 | 7 | 2 | 500 |
| Croswell & Harvey, | Ohio | Gregory's Gulch, | June 15, | Two Mule Power, | 14 | 2 | 7 | 2 | 500 |
| Travers & Hill, | Ohio | Nevada Gulch, | July 10, | " | | 2 | 7 | 2 | 500 |
| Keene & Miller, | Tenn | " | July 1, | " | | 2 | 6 | 2 | 500 |
| J. F. Place & Co., | | Russell's Gulch, | | " | | 1 | 9 | 4 | 500 |
| Farmington & Rogers, | | " | | " | 1 | 1 | 8½ | 4 | 500 |
| Austin Smith, | Ia. | Utilla Creek, | June 22, | " | 1 | 7 | 2 | 150 | |
| See Appendix No. 7. | | | | | | | | | |

# GUIDE TO THE GOLD MINES.

## TABLE OF DISTANCES.

### FROM OMAHA TO DENVER CITY.

#### OMAHA.

MILES.

From this city a large emigration starts annually for the Gold Fields of the Rocky Mountains. The sloughs, creeks and rivers are well bridged between this city and Fort Kearney. It is thickly settled for 200 miles. The Hannibal and St. Joseph Railroad have a line of packets running between St. Joseph and this city, thus facilitating Eastern travel.

The following table does not give the names of all Ranches on the route, but merely those that have accommodations for emigrants, and those that have made calculations to meet the wants of the emigration. As they are the only *reliable* ranches on the route, emigrants and others will do well to camp as convenient to them as possible. One mile from Omaha, will find good accommodations at C. S. MORRIS' Ranche, where they can have their stock well cared for..................1

LITTLE PAPILLON.—Water and grass..................8
PAPILLON.—Water and grass..................4
REED'S RANCH.—Plenty of hay and stabling; water and grass and good camping..................3
J. F. MUNGER.—Hay, corn and good stabling. General accommodations..................8
ELKHORN CITY.—A small settlement here. Good accommodations for emigrants and stock can be obtained at the City Hotel, kept by Mr. Robinson and Mrs. Barber..................8

## GUIDE TO THE GOLD MINES.

MILES

BRIDGEPORT.—Situated on the Elkhorn River, one mile from Elkhorn City. Several stores and large settlement. Those wishing to camp here for the night, can find good accommodations for themselves and excellent stabling for their stock, at the McNeal House, the last house before crossing Elkhorn bridge. Plenty of wood, water and grass. From here a long prairie is crossed, occasionally passing water in sloughs; in wet weather the road is bad..................................1
FARMER'S HOUSE—by Reuben Kissel. General accommodations. Plenty of water and grass........................................ 11½
FREMONT.—A large settlement; several stores, etc..............8
NYE'S HOTEL.—Nye & Colson, proprietors. General accommodations. The largest stable between Omaha and Denver..................
VALLEY HOUSE—by Margaret Turner. W. S. Co's station. Good hotel accommodations; stabling; corn and hay for sale....................
DALE HOUSE—kept by W. R. Hazen. Corn meal, oats, hay and stabling at moderate prices. Good camping ground...................8
NORTH BEND.—River View House. This is a good camping ground. Here the Platte strikes the road. Plenty of wood, water and grass. Mr. Morrison, of the River View House, keeps a good hotel, good stabling. Hay and corn for sale at reasonable rates. .......................12
RANCHE and Store, W. H. Ely, proprietor.............................1½
PLATTE VALLEY HOUSE—by Robert Graham. Hay, corn, stabling, blacksmithing, wood, water and grass ............................1½
BUCHANAN HOUSE—at Shell creek, by Nelson Toncrey. Wood water and grass. Good camping ground. Hay and corn for sale ........ 7½
ALEXANDER ALBERTSON keeps hay and corn for sale; stabling. Good camping ground. One mile west of Shell creek.................. 1
66 MILE HOUSE—from Omaha; kept by Heinrich Ralfer. General accommodations. Hay, corn and pork for sale. Good water and grass...............................................................5
JUNCTION RANCHE—by H. Bushnell. General accommodations for emigrants and stock. Here is a blacksmith shop where all kinds of making and repairing can be done on short notice. Wood, water, and grass ...........................................................2½
JOSEPH RUSSEL'S.—Plenty of wood, water and grass. Accommodations for emigrants and stock....................................½
PETER MURIE keeps for sale hay, corn, corn meal, flour and potatoes. Good camping ground and good roads.....................10
JAMES GALLEY'S.—Hay, corn and stabling. Good camping ground. Wood, water and grass ...................................... ½

### COLUMBUS
is situated on the north branch of the Loupe Fork. Ferry crosses here. Those wishing to replenish their outfit in any particular, can do so

GUIDE TO THE GOLD MINES. 59

MILES

at the store of F. G. Beeher, who keeps a general assortment of groceries. Likewise will be found here, the offices of the Western Stage Company, United States Express Company, and the Post Office. Good stabling; hay and corn for sale. Messrs. Rickey & Co., on the south side of the road, also keeps a good assortment of everything necessary for the emigrant; also, all kinds of meat for sale. At the American Hotel, kept by R. C. Baker, travelers can regale themselves with a good meal of victuals, a comfortable bed, and good stabling for stock, at moderate prices. This is the W. S. Co. station. By reference to the Ferry Company's advertisement, emigrants can there see rates of toll............................................................3

After crossing Loupe Fork Ferry the next ranche is
GUY C. BARNUM'S.—Hay and corn for sale. W. S. Co. station. Good camping ground...................................................................1
PRAIRIE CREEK RANCHE—by Henry Hurley. Good accommodations for emigrants and stock. Prairie creek is bridged..................11
JAMES CUMMINS'.—W. S. Co. station........................................9
W. H. HUFTALEN'S.—Sign of the "Red, White and Blue." Store; good stabling; good camping ground. Here is where the road from Genoa Ferry again strikes the Platte.............................................6
Those wishing to go by the way of Genoa, will keep up the north side of Loupe Fork to Patrick Murray's, where corn, hay and stabling can be obtained...........................................................................4
GERRARD'S RANCHE—on Looking-glass creek. Good camping ground; hay, corn and general accommodations.....................................8
CHARLES SAUNDER'S.—General accommodations, groceries, provisions, hay and corn. Good camping........................................8
GENOA, Platte County. A large settlement with stores and Post Office. Within half a mile of the Indian Reservation. Good crossing and ferriage. Emigrants can obtain supplies here at the store of Daniel Walsh, or at the store of Henry J. Hudson, who keep a general assortment of groceries. W. G. and J. L. Bowman, Indian traders, keep a large assortment of furs, robes and peltries; they have always a large stock of horses and stock for sale and trade. Their store is quarter of a mile north of the Genoa ferry. After crossing the ferry you travel over a prairie of 16 miles, when you again strike the Platte and join the road that is traveled from Columbus................................3
JASON H. PARKER'S.—General accommodations. Hay and corn for sale. Good camping ground....................................................8
LONE TREE RANCH—by T. J. Marmoy. Groceries, hay, corn and stabling. On the bank of the Platte..............................................8
W. S. CO. STATION—by Samuel G. Hayward. Good camping ground.......................................................................................1

E. D. HURLEY'S.—Groceries. Stock of any kind kept for twenty-five cents per day per span......................................................9½

JESSE SHOEMAKER'S POINT.—General accommodations and good camping ground..................................................................½

JAMES VIEREGG'S RANCH.—Corn and hay for sale. Good camping ground.............................................................................5

BARNARD'S RANCH.—Hay and corn for sale. Here, there is a German settlement. A large crop of grain was raised the past year, and corn can be obtained at from 70 to 90 cents per bushel...............5½

E. D. BUCK & CO.—Groceries. Hay and corn for sale, and good camping ground..................................................................5

CROCKER'S RANCHE.—Hotel accommodations, store, and good camping ground. This is the mouth of Wood river, a clear stream with plenty of Timber and good grass................................................1

M. TOWNSLEY'S.—Wood river saw-mill. General accommodations. On the opposite side of the road is a drug store kept by Dr. Sales...........1

W. S. CO. STATION—by Squire Lamb. Good camping ground..........1

W. G. ELDRIDGE'S.—Good camping ground and general accommodations.................................................................................5

MILLER & CO'S RANCHE.—Potatoes, hay, corn and general accommodations.................................................................................4

P. MOORE.—Corralle, general accommodations and good camping.......2

COTTONWOOD LAWN RANCHE—by James Jackson. Hay, corn and stabling............................................................................2

CHARLES HUYLER'S RANCHE.—Stabling, wood, water and grass....2

THOMAS PAGE'S RANCHE.—Corn, hay and stabling. Good camping ground...........................................................................½

WOOD RIVER CENTRE.—Post office and store. The *Huntsman's Echo* is published here by J. E. Johnson. Corn for sale....................1

COBBLER'S RANCH—by Edward Oliver. Provisions, wood, water and grass............................................................................½

PECK, ROBERTSON & CO.—Dry goods, groceries and provisions. Blacksmith shop. Good camping ground, and corn for sale..............1½

JOHN EVANS.—General accommodations, wood, water and grass.....2½

CALVIN THOMPSON'S RANCH.—General accommodations and good camping ground.............................................................2

C. H. WILSON'S RANCHE.—Farm and stabling. Corn for sale and good camping. On bank of Wood River..........................................½

BOYD BROTHERS.—Nebraska Centre Post office. Groceries; good stabling. Brewery and blacksmith shop.........................................1½

TOUSLEY, McLAIN & CROSS.—General accommodations and good camping ground. Hay for sale..............................................7

MILLER & CO'S RANCHE.—Hay, corn, stabling and general accommodations. On the bank of the Platte, at the crossing. Here the river is divided by several islands, and is about two miles in width; difficult crossing at high water........................................................2

FORT KEARNEY.—Emigrants can obtain supplies from the sutlers. John Heath & Co's store is on the main traveled road to Denver. The Telegraph office is located in the Fort Kearney news depot, where all the latest papers and periodicals can be obtained. The Post office is in the same building. Mr. Sydenham, Postmaster.........................2

At certain seasons of the year, the Platte is difficult to ford at this point. Two miles from here is

## KEARNEY CITY.

It has got a population of about 300; is neatly laid off, and is situated in the centre of a sea of prairie. To the south of Kearney City lays a long range of mountains, and on the north, is the Platte, with its large bodies of timber, which promise the citizens an abundant supply of fuel. A large number of business men seeing its advantageous position, have located here, and brought with them large stocks of goods, which they offer to sell at a slight advance on Eastern prices. The following are the names and locations of business men:

### NORTH SIDE OF ROAD.

JOHN TALBOT—first store on north side of road. Mr. Talbot is one of the oldest settlers, and one of the first business men in the city. He keeps a general assortment of everything necessary for the emigrant. Connected with his establishment is a bakery, where there can be obtained everything in that line. A ten-pin alley is now added to the establishment.

CLARK & SIMPSON.—Restaurant and Saloon. The saloon is well stocked with good liquors, and the restaurant will be supplied with all the delicacies of the season.

SELDON, NICHOLSON & CO.—(Sign of the American Flag.) General outfitting. The largest corralle in the country. Blacksmithing of all kinds done with dispatch.

### SOUTH SIDE OF ROAD.

CLAYES & MOREHEAD.—General assortment of groceries. Hay and corn for sale. Good stabling.

PECK, ROBERTSON & Co.—Dry goods, groceries and general outfitting. Blacksmith shop.

JOHN HOLLAND.—Cheap cash store. General assortment of provisions and groceries.

McDONALD & YOUNG.—Sign of the Elk horn. General outfitting, hotel and corralle. W. S. Co's office.

JOHN BUTLER keeps a general assortment of groceries, liquors and everything in his line.

MILES

SAMUEL WALSH—dealer in groceries, provisions, liquors, hay and corn. Feed for sale. Attached is a first class eating house, where meals, got up in a proper style, can be obtained at all times. Pure liquors and cigars will be found at the bar.

From Kearney City the road continues good until you reach
    FRANCIS BEERMAN'S—one mile west of Kearney. Groceries; bakery; corralle. Hay and corn for sale. Good water and grass..........1
    EIGHT MILE POINT—by Thomas Keeler. Groceries, hay and corn. Good corralle. ...........................................................................6
    YOUNG & CO'S RANCHE.—Groceries, and accommodations for emigrants. Water and grass; wood at a short distance....................8½
    C. O. C. & P. P. EX. CO'S STATION.—Kept by Mr. Correston.........3½
    SYDENHAM'S RANCHE.—Hope Town. Hay, corn, groceries and corralle. Water and grass..................................................................8½
    IOWA RANCHE—by Joseph Gardiner. Corralle, stabling, wood, water and grass..............................................................................3
    DAVIDSON'S RANCHE.—Good corralle, wood, water and grass. Good road.............................................................................................3
    25 MILE RANCHE—kept by Fred Smith. Flour, groceries, bacon, hay and corn for sale.............................................................................8
    FINLEY BURTCH'S RANCHE.—Provisions for sale. Good grass. Platte river at a short distance from the road..........................................4
    PLUM CREEK—a clear stream about eight feet wide, here enters into the Platte. There are two ranches here, without supplies................6
    C. O. C. & P. P. EX. CO'S STATION...................................................1
    JAMES PARSONS'.—Groceries, hay and corn; corralle....................2
    JOHN SHARP'S.—Groceries. Corn for sale. Corralle and stabling. Wood, water and grass. Road good ....................................................2
    FREEMAN'S RANCHE—by Daniel Freeman. Groceries and provisions. Water and grass...........................................................................8
    RANCHE.—Charge exhorbitant prices...............................................9
    SMITH'S RANCHE.—Good water and grass, plenty of timber. Groceries. Good corralle. W. S. Co's station ........................................9
    C. O. C. & P. P. EX. CO'S STATION. ...........................................10
    SPRINGVILLE RANCHE.—Trading post. Entertainment for travelers. Several good springs, plenty of grass, some timber on the Platte.....4
    McDONALD & CLARK'S RANCHE and Store. Good corralle and stabling. Plenty of water and grass..................................................13
    CAPITOLA CITY.—J. Mechatt's trading post. Groceries, buffalo robes, furs and skins for sale. Corn and hay. Good corralle and excellent camping ground..........................................................................5

### COTTONWOOD SPRINGS.

Several business houses are located here. From a distance this place has a very picturesque appearance; from the town a magnificent view of the Platte is presented. South of the village runs a continuous line of bluffs, which protects it from the sweeping prairie winds. A large belt of timber back of the bluffs affords abundant fuel for the use of the settlers.

Emigrants wishing to recruit their supplies, can do so at the store of CORMEIL PILKA—who keeps an assortment of groceries.
ISADORE P. BOYER.—Groceries and provisions. West side of road.
CHARLES MCDONALD.—Groceries, dry goods, bacon, corn, hay and an excellent corralle. W. S. Co's station. Entertainment for travelers......9

BALDWIN, PEGRAM & CO.—Large stock of flour and groceries of all kinds. Good water and grass........................................................2
HAYS & BROTHERS.—Groceries and provisions. Good camping ground..........................................................................................1
W. M. HINMAN.—Ranche and blacksmith shop. About one mile northwest of Hays & Brothers, on the river road. Excellent camping ground..........................................................................................1
JUNCTION RANCHE—by J. A. Morrows. Trading post. Good assortment of groceries, dry goods, hardware, etc., Water, grass and good corralle. This is known as the half-way house between Omaha and Denver. Free bridge..............................................................2
FREMONT SLOUGH.—Ranche kept by W. Bischopf. Groceries and wood for sale. Water and grass. W. S. Co's station.....................11
FREMONT SPRINGS.—P. P. EX. CO'S STATION......................9
'After passing over a high rolling prairie, a steep precipitous sand ridge is crossed, which again brings you to the Platte, this is known as
O'FALLON'S BLUFFS.—Here is Williams' ranche, where emigrants can obtain supplies. A blacksmith shop is attached where repairing is done on reasonable terms..................................................................8
MOORE'S RANCHE.—Mr. Moore has got one of the best assorted stocks to be found on the road. His charges are reasonable, and he has everything that emigrants require. Mr. M. has 300 tons of hay, which he has been selling at one dollar per hundred. Parties wishing to sell, trade or exchange stock, will here find a good variety to select from. W. S. Co's station. A blacksmith shop is located here, and all repairing is promptly attended to. Large corralle................................8
DORSEY'S RANCHE.—Groceries and bakery. Good water and grass, and good roads..........................................................................2
C. O. C. & P. P. EX. CO'S STATION....................................26
DIAMOND SPRINGS.—P. P. Ex. Co's station. Roads good..........26
BEAUVAIS.—Trading post and ranche. Lower Platte crossing. A large assortment of Indian goods, furs, robes, &c. Groceries. W. F. Lee, Agent. Good camping ground....................................................8

## GUIDE TO THE GOLD MINES.

BAKER & FALES.—Buckeye ranche. W. S. Co's station. Groceries and provisions. Road good........................2
SAND CREEK RANCHE.—Walden & Horner. Hay, corn, flour and wood for sale..............................
Some heavy sand bluffs to be crossed between here and GALESBURGH.—Upper crossing of the Platte. Post office and express station. Pony express crosses the river here. A store is kept by Messrs. Chrisman & Thompson, where everything that emigrants require may be obtained. Good camping ground........................12
NEBRASKA RANCHE.—Ackley & Forbes. W. S. Co's station. Hay, corn, flour, groceries and stabling. Water and grass. Wood for sale. Heavy sand for two miles.........................6
TWELVE MILE RANCHE.—Simons & Hafford. Hay, corn and groceries for sale. Good water and grass........................14
SPRING HILL.—C. O. C. & P. P. Ex. Co's station........................5
LILLIAN SPRINGS RANCHE.—W. S. Co's station. Store; corralle. Good water and grass. Heavy sand........................21
C. O. C. & P. P. EX. CO'S STATION.—Store and groceries. Occasional heavy sands. W. A. Kelley........................21
H. GODFREY & CO.—Groceries and bakery. All kinds of Vegetables can be obtained here. Good water and grass........................5
STEVENS & MOORE.—Beaver Creek Ranche. C. O. C. & P. P. Ex. Co's station. Groceries and general accommodations. Roads good........................23
WM. McMACKIN & CO.—W. S. Co's station. General accomodations. Bakery. Good water and grass........................2½
FRED. LAMB.—C. O. C. & P. P. Ex. Co's station. Hay for sale. Meals at all hours. Roads good........................½
A half mile from here is what is now generally known as the

### "CUT OFF TO DENVER."

It is now an acknowledged fact that this is the best road, not only in point of travel, but it is sixty miles shorter than the Platte road. A large number of the heavy teams that freight between the Missouri River and Denver pass over this road, thus satisfying the credulous that it must have decided preference over the Platte route. It is a Toll road, (I believe the toll is one dollar per team.) Considerable dispute has been occasioned by emigrants and others denying the right of collecting toll. This right has been tried by the legal courts of Denver City, and they have in all cases decided in favor of Col. N. D. Morris, the gentleman who received the charter from the Kansas and Nebraska Legislatures to levy toll by this road. The first ranche come to, is

BIJOU RANCHE, kept by Col. N. D. Morris. General accommodations. Wood water and grass. One mile of sand..................................13
C. O. C. & P. P. EX. CO'S STATION, kept by V. Wood. Water and grass...................................................................................15
Here you again strike a high bluff; the road is now rolling, until you reach LIVING SPRINGS. Good water and plenty of grass..........15
Road is rolling until you reach KIOWA RANCHE, kept by H. Conant. Plenty of water and grass..........................................................6
BOX ELDER.—Hay for sale. C. O. C. & P. P. Co's station. Kept by H. Conant.................................................................................0
EIGHT MILE CREEK.—Col. N. D. Morris. Hay for sale. Here the toll gate is located, where those having to pass over the road will be waited on by Mr. Morris, or his agents. Water and grass.............13
DENVER CITY.................................................................................8

## DISTANCES ON DENVER, MT. VERNON TOLL ROAD TO GREGORY'S DIGGINGS.

From Denver City to MOUNT VERNON HOUSE, by A. G. Morrison, Mt. Vernon......................................................................................15
GREGORY'S DIGGINGS..................................................................19

## DISTANCES FROM DENVER CITY TO GREGORY MINES, BY GOLDEN CITY.

MINERS' HOTEL.—Golden City.......................................................15
GOLDEN GATE..................................................................................2
EIGHT MILE HOUSE.—Robinson and Baker. Good water. Ranche. From here you ascend a steep canon, until you reach the top of a very steep mountain; great care will have to be taken to properly block your wagon. This mountain is half-a-mile from the top to the to the bottom. Half-a-mile from the foot of the hill is........................6
GUY'S HOTEL.....................................................................................2
GREGORY MINES.............................................................................12

## DISTANCES FROM DENVER CITY TO TARRYALL CITY AND CANON CITY.

BRADFORD.......................................................................................14
OHIO VALLEY HOUSE—by A. B. Adams. Plenty of wood, grass and water. Good accommodations.....................................................17

MILES

From here you go over a hilly and very rough road, until the South Park is reached, which is five miles wide and fifteen miles long; in summer there is a bountiful supply of grass and water for stock. At the south-western end is

TARRYALL.—This city, situated in the centre of what is known as the *Tarryall Diggings*, has now a population of about 400; has several hotels, stores, express offices, &c. Its position in connection with the surrounding country, is such, that it must ultimately be the depot for that vast country whose riches and mineral resources are yet in their infancy. Parties going to Canon City, California Gulch and the San Juan mines, pass through here. Rich quartz mines are being opened, and quartz mills erected in the immediate vicinity, which will be the means of building and concentrating a business capital at Tarryall, which will make its effects felt throughout the mining regions. The "Town Company" offer great inducements to mechanics and business men making their locations here.................................................30

CANON CITY.—This is a flourishing young city. Its position places it in direct connection with the new gold fields of New Mexico. The *Canon City Times*, a neat and sprightly paper, is published here by H. S. Millet, Esq. ...........................................................75

# BUSINESS DIRECTORY OF DENVER CITY.

*The following are the names of the largest and most prominent Professional and Business Houses in this city. On account of the many changes in locations, it is not deemed necessary to give them.*

## DENVER CITY.

The commercial emporium of the Rocky Mountain Gold Regions is situated on the north side of the South Platte, fifteen miles below where the latter makes its exit from the mountains. The growth of Denver is unparalleled in the history of western town building.

Its actual population at the present time is 7,000. Here are established branches of the most extensive business houses in the West. Several large brick buildings have been erected within the past year. There are three newspapers published here, viz: the Rocky Mountain *Herald*, daily and weekly, published by Thomas Gibson; the *Mountaineer*, daily and weekly, and the Rocky Mountain *News*, daily and weekly, published by the "News Printing Co."

Below will be found the advertisements of the most responsible business, and professional men in the city, to which we invite your particular attention.

GROCERIES & PROVISIONS.
BRUCE & CO., Cushman, Agent.
GERRISH & CO. See adv.
J. Garnhart.
Fisher & Co.
J. H. VOORHEIS.
B. F. Carr.
GREENLEAF & BREWER, see adv.
J. W. Smith.
H. MURDOCH. See adv.
William Dunn.
BUDDEE & JACOBS. See adv.
BALDWIN, PEGRAM & CO.

DRY GOODS AND GROCERIES.
J. B. DOYLE & CO. See adv.
A. P. Vasquez.
DOLD & CO. See adv.
Hatch & Co.
J. M. & C. W. Railey.

C. ST. VRAIN. See adv.
Simon Cort.
Wallingford & Co.

DRY GOODS, CLOTHING, ETC.
Clayton, Lowe & Co.
STETTAUER & CO.
Fenton & Purcell.
ALEX. MAJORS.

MERCHANTS AND FREIGHTERS.
JONES & CARTWRIGHT. See adv.
ALEX. MAJORS. See adv.
Hiram Lightner.
R. B. Bradford.
BALDWIN, PEGRAM & CO.
T. Richards.

AUCTION AND COMMISSION.
C. A. COOKE & CO.
Charles Collins.

Burton & Higgins.
C. H. Keith.
Cooke & Collins.

### ARCHITECTS AND SURVEYORS.
MOODY & MARION. See adv.
Buell & Boyd.

### REAL ESTATE.
WHITSITT & WILDMAN. See adv.
J. H. DUDLEY & CO. See vdy.
A. C. HUNT & CO. See adv.
G. Wynkoop & Co.

### ATTORNEYS AT LAW.
PURKINS & WELD.
H. R. Hunt.
D. C. Collier.
S. W. Wagoner.
H. P. Bennett.
J. C. Moore.
W. P. McClure.
J. H. Sherman.
— Downing.

### NOTARIES PUBLIC.
D. C. Collier.
F. A. Hunt.
G. Wynkoop.
J. B. Atkins.

### BOOTS AND SHOES.
T. C. Willard.
Kerr & Soule.
J. W. Todd.
J. M. Parker.

### PHYSICIANS AND SURGEONS.
J. J. SAVILLE. See adv.
H. H. Beals.
O. D. CASS.
— Hamilton.
— Furbringer.
A. Steinberger.
A. F. Peck.
D. Griswold.
W. M. Belt.

### STORAGE AND COMMISSION.
BUDDEE & JACOBS. See adv.
C. A. COOKE & CO. See adv.
J. H. VOORHEIS. See adv.
Byers, Devon & Co.

### CONTRACTORS AND BUILDERS.
J. B. Ashard.
Maine & Chandler.
W. E. Travers.

### CABINET AND CHAIR FACTORIES.
Moyer & Rice.
McGain & Walley.
J. B. Stockton.

### DRUGGISTS AND APOTHECARIES.
W. Graham.
E. F. Cheeseman.
H. H. Hewitt.

### HOTELS.
TREMONT HOUSE,
 by Seargent & Bradford. See adv.
BROADWELL HOUSE.
CHEROKEE HOUSE,
  by Crocker & ——
Vasquez House,
  by Thompson & Barnes.
Jefferson House, by Carr & Piles.

### RESTAURANTS.
T. Digby.
Hawkins & Wicks.
Cherokee House.

### BOARDING HOUSES.
Winterset House, J. B. Bell.
Chicago House, D. Andrews.
Kansas House, L. Silverthrow.
Penn House, T. Buttles.
Idaho House, A. B. Moore.
Mrs. Lane, Larimer street.

### HARDWARE.
NYE, BRADLEY & CO. See adv.

### STABLES AND RANCHE.
Teats & Co.

### BAKERS.
F. MARK, Chicago Bakery.
A. Fall & Co.
Hawkins & Co., St. Louis Bakery.
Harris & Hemphill.
C. Hest.

### MERCHANT TAILORS.
FRANCIS FARREL, Blake street.

### CLOTHING AND DRY GOODS.
STETTAUER & BRO. See adv.
T. Rothschild.
B. F. DALTON.
L. Myers & Co.

### HARNESS MAKERS.
Wood & Railey.
J. A. Hills.
J. Landis.

**BOOK STORE.**
WOOLWORTH & MOFFATT.

**AMBROTYPES.**
— Bricker.

**TRADERS—GENERAL.**
E. H. Hart.
Peter Turley.

**WAGON AND CARRIAGE MAKERS.**
Wright & Weldon.

**SOAP AND CANDLE MANUFACTURER.**
Miller, Perry & Co.

**PLANING MILL.**
Cherry Creek.

**FOUNDRY.**
Scoville & Co.

**EXCHANGE OFFICE.**
Pollard's Exchange.

**EXPRESS—PASSENGER AND FREIGHT.**
C. O. C. & P. P. Ex. Co. See adv.
HINCKLEY & CO.
Western Stage Co.
Pease & Co.
Howe, Fair & Co.
JOHN P. BRUCE & Co. See adv.

**MILLINERY AND DRESS MAKING.**
Mrs. A. R. Palmer.
Mrs. Cody.
M. Davis.
Mrs. Parker.

**WASHING AND IRONING.**
Mrs. Welch, Larimer street.
Mary Calvin (colored).

**BANKING HOUSES.**
CLARK, GRUBER & CO., (Mint).
TURNER & HOBBS.
CASS, WILCOX & CO.
Brown Bros. & Co.

**TIN SMITHS.**
Kenna & Nye.
G. W. Merk.
F. Crawford.

**PRINTING OFFICES.**
ROCKY MOUNTAIN NEWS, D. and W.
Rocky Mountain Herald, D. and W.
Denver Mountaineer, D. and W.

**LIQUORS—WHOLESALE.**
J. H. Voorheis.

C. E. & E. A. Tilton.
Geo. E. Bayard.
Geo. F. Boengesser.
Loeb & Klingstein.
W. E. House.

**BILLIARD SALOONS.**
Simon & Seeman, (Metropolitan).
J. H. Ming & Co. (International).
Barnes & Gunnell, (Apollo).

**LIVERY STABLES.**
Summers & Co.
— Palmer.

**BLACKSMITHS.**
C. Harris.
Powers & Owens.
J. Wisner.
T. Pollock.

**WATCHMAKERS.**
W. J. HOWARD. See adv.
W. R. Roath.
S. C. Gallup.

**LUMBER.**
S. H. MOER & CO.
— Fisher.
Oaks & Co.
Travilla & Willhite.
Hogeboon & Co.
Bowery & Eastridge.

**GUNSMITHS.**
S. Hawken.
Henderson & Andrews.
H. Hitchens.

**BUTCHERS.**
Dan'l Ullman.
Shaw, Bailey & Co.
Ormstein & Marshal.
Buttrick & Co.

**BARBERS.**
J. G. Smith.
C. Bartholomew.
E. J. Sanderlin.
H. Murat.

**CIGARS, TOBACCO AND PIPES.**
HAAS & BROS. See adv.
Simon, Secman & Co.
J. H. Snedecor.
H. J. Brendlinger.

**PAINTERS.**
Henderson & Andrews.
H. Hutchins.

# BOOK STORE

—AND—

## NEWS DEPOT.

### WOOLWORTH & MOFFAT,

DEALERS IN

## BOOKS, STATIONERY,

### WALL PAPER,

NEWSPAPERS AND PERIODICALS,

**DENVER,** □ □ **JEFFERSON.**

WE KEEP EVERYTHING USUALLY FOR SALE IN

**FIRST CLASS, WIDE AWAKE BOOK STORES**

SPECIAL AGENTS

—FOR—

☞ **SCHOOL BOOKS.** ☜

By especial arrangement we are enabled to supply the very latest Eastern Newspapers at all times, and in advance of the mails.

A. M. CLARK.   E. H. GRUBER.   M. E. CLARK.

## CLARK, GRUBER & CO.,
# BANKERS.

DEALERS IN EXCHANGE, CURRENCY AND GOLD DUST,

DEPOSITS RECEIVED.

**Denver City, and Leavenworth, Kansas.**

We draw on AMERICAN EXCHANGE BANK, New York; ALLEN, COPP & NESBIT, St. Louis; GILMORE, DUNLAP & Co., Cincinnati; MARINE BANK, Chicago, and CLARK, GRUBER & Co., Leavenworth City.

We have in connection with Banking, a MINT, and are prepared to exchange our coin for Gold Dust. The native gold is coined as it is found, alloyed with silver. The weight will be greater, but the value the same as the United States coin of like denomination.

**CLARK, GRUBER & CO., Denver City.**

---

U. TURNER.   TURNER & HOBBS,   J. HOBBS.

# BANKERS,

## OFFICE, ON FERRY STREET, - -' WEST DENVER.

**REFERENCES:**

BENEDICT & CO,    -    -    - New York. | W. H. BARKSDALE & CO.,   -   St. Louis.
DUNCAN, SHERMAN & CO.,      "    "    | UNION BANK,    -    -    -    -    "

---

O. D. CASS.   C. H. WILCOX.   J. B. CASS.

# EXCHANGE BANK
—OF—
# CASS, WILCOX & CO.,

## DEALERS IN GOLD DUST, COIN AND EXCHANGE,

**Blake Street, corner F & G Street, Denver, Kansas.**

**REFERENCES:**

JONES & CARTWRIGHT,   - Denver City | A. BEATTIE & CO.,   -   -   - St. Joseph, Mo.
THOMAS CARNEY,   - Leavenworth, K. T | J. J. ANDERSON & CO.,   -   - St. Louis, Mo.
BANK OF CHENANGO,   - Norwich, N. Y | AMERICAN EXCHANGE BANK, New York.

---

J. H. VOORHEIS,

# STORAGE AND COMMISSION

DEALER IN

## GROCERIES, PROVISIONS, ETC.

**FERRY STREET, Opposite Jefferson House,   -   -   DENVER.**

| JOHN P. BRUCE, | L. S. HOWE, | SAMUEL CUSHMAN, Jr. |
| St. Joseph, Mo. | St. Joseph, Mo. | Denver City, J. T. |

## JNO. P. BRUCE & Co.,

Express and General

FREIGHTERS

From ST. JOSEPH, Missouri,

To DENVER and the MINES.

**EXPRESS FREIGHT TRANSPORTED BY MULE TRAINS IN QUICK TIME AND AT LOW RATES.**

TRAINS RUNNING THROUGHOUT THE YEAR.

Cattle Trains leave St. Joseph every month of the Summer season.

ALSO, WHOLESALE AND RETAIL DEALERS
—IN—

IRON, HARDWARE

AND

PROVISIONS,

DENVER CITY, ▫ ▫ JEFFERSON.

Consignments Solicited.   Commissions Low.

**Warehouse in Denver, on Fifth street, between Front and Cherry streets.**
**Office in St. Joseph, at the Journal Office, on Second street.**

# JONES & CARTWRIGHT,

## PIKE'S PEAK

# TRANSPORTATION LINE

**FREIGHTS TRANSPORTED TO ALL POINTS in the MINES**

Trains leave weekly from St. Joseph, Leavenworth and Atchison for Denver City and the Mines.

☞ Goods forwarded without delay.

JONES & CARTWRIGHT,
DENVER CITY.

---

# C. A. COOK & CO.,
### (FIRE PROOF WAREHOUSE.)

# Commission Merchants
## AND GENERAL STORAGE.

DEALERS IN

# GROCERIES AND PROVISIONS,
### BOOTS AND SHOES, ETC.

## BLAKE STREET,
One Door from F Street. }    **DENVER CITY.**

☞ LIBERAL ADVANCES MADE ON ALL CONSIGNMENTS. ☜

**REFERENCES:**

| | |
|---|---|
| McMECHAN & BALLANTINE, Wholesale Grocers and Commission Merchants, | St. Louis |
| JOHN J. ANDERSON & CO., Bankers, | St. Louis |
| CLARK, GRUBER & CO., Bankers, | Leavenworth City |
| SCOTT, KERR & CO., " | Leavenworth City |

N. SARGENT. - - - - - - GEORGE C. BRADFORD.

# TREMONT HOUSE,

—BY—

## SARGENT & BRADFORD,

### FRONT STREET,

Head of Blake Street. } DENVER CITY.

---

A. BUDDEE.        A. JACOBS.

## BUDDEE & JACOBS,

### Forwarding and Commission

## MERCHANTS,

AND DEALERS IN

### GROCERIES AND PROVISIONS,

### DENVER, J. T.

---

REFER TO

| | | | |
|---|---|---|---|
| ROBERT CAMPBELL & CO., | - St. Louis. | C. C. WOOLWORTH, - - | St. Joseph |
| J. A. HORBACH & CO., - - | - Omaha, | RUSSELL, MAJORS & WADDEL, | Denver |
| JONES & CARTWRIGHT, - | - Denver. | R. B. BRADFORD & CO., - - | " |
| J. B. DOYLE & CO., - | - " | TURNER & HOBBS, - - - - | " |

J. DOLD & BROTHER.     A. HANAUER.

# DOLD & CO.,

**WHOLESALE AND RETAIL DEALERS IN**

**FAMILY AND FANCY**

# GROCERIES

FOREIGN AND DOMESTIC

## LIQUORS,

## HARDWARE, TINWARE,

**MINING TOOLS,**

## BOOTS AND SHOES,

## CLOTHING,

**HATS AND CAPS, Etc.**

COR. FIFTH AND FERRY STREETS,

DENVER, J. T.

# GREENLEAF & BREWER,

**NEW BRICK BUILDING,**

## LARIMER STREET,

BETWEEN E AND F STREETS.     DENVER CITY.

DEALERS IN

## GROCERIES, PROVISIONS,

### HARDWARE,

MINING AND FARMING IMPLEMENTS

CHOICE WINES and LIQUORS,

CIGARS, ETC.

### STORAGE AND COMMISSION.

GOODS STORED AT REASONABLE RATES, AND SOLD ON COMMISSION IF DESIRED.

GREENLEAF & BREWER.

## GERRISH & CO.,

WHOLESALE DEALERS IN

## Provisions, Groceries,

## LIQUORS,

—AND—

OUTFITTING GOODS OF EVERY DESCRIPTION.

CORNER OF F AND M'GAA STREETS,

DENVER CITY, ▫ ▫ JEFFERSON.

---

## J. B. DOYLE & CO.,

DEALERS IN FANCY AND

## FAMILY GROCERIES

FOREIGN AND DOMESTIC LIQUORS,

## HARDWARE, TINWARE

MINING TOOLS,

BOOTS, SHOES, CLOTHING, HATS, CAPS,

OILS, PAINTS, ETC.

**CORNER OF FERRY AND FIFTH STREETS,**

J. B. DOYLE,
FRED Z. SALOMON, }        DENVER.

## C. ST. VRAIN,

**WHOLESALE AND RETAIL DEALER IN**

## FLOUR,

## Family and Fancy Groceries

### BOOTS AND SHOES,

### HATS AND CAPS, CLOTHING,

#### TINWARE,

### Hardware and Mining Tools

Blake Street, between F and G Streets,

**DENVER CITY.**

---

## BALDWIN, PEGRAM & CO.,

**DEALERS IN**

## PROVISIONS

AND

## FLOUR,

BLAKE STREET, OPPOSITE THE BOXED TREES,

**DENVER, JEFFERSON.**

LEWIS N. TAPPAN, late of Kansas.　　　GEORGE H. TAPPAN, late of Boston.

# TAPPAN & CO.,
# GENERAL COMMISSION MERCHANTS

### WHOLESALE AND RETAIL DEALERS IN

# GROCERIES, PROVISIONS,

## RUBBER HOSE, BELTING, BOOTS AND SHOES

### HATS AND CAPS,

# FORCE PUMPS, SAFES, NOTIONS

—AND—

## MINER'S OUTFITS.

### DENVER AND COLORADO CITIES, · · · JEFFERSON.

REFERENCES:

| | | | |
|---|---|---|---|
| TAPPAN & McBURNEY, | - - Boston. | F. W. TAPPAN, - - - | New York. |
| HENRY N. HOOPER & CO. | - " | WM. H. CARY, - - - | " |
| BAILY & CO., - - - | - Philadelphia. | GOODRICH, WILLARD & CO., | St. Louis. |

C. J. COWHERD.　　J. F. TAYLOR.　　R. R. WHITE.　　C. PREVOST.

# TAYLOR, WHITE & CO.,

## Storage and Commission Merchants

### AND DEALERS IN

# GROCERIES

—AND—

# PROVISIONS,

## CORNER OF BLAKE AND F STREETS,

### DENVER CITY.

# H. MURDOCK,

Wholesale and Retail Dealer in

## FANCY AND FAMILY GROCERIES,

Foreign and Domestic Liquors,

HARDWARE, TINWARE, MINING TOOLS,

BOOTS AND SHOES,

CLOTHING, HATS, CAPS, ETC.

LARIMER ST., between F. and G. Sts., DENVER.

---

ALEX. MAJORS,

And Wholesale Dealer in

## Groceries and Provisions,

HARDWARE,

CLOTHING, BOOTS AND SHOES,

At Cost and Transportation.

ALEX. MAJORS,

FERRY STREET, next door to Turner and Hobbs' Bank, in the Fire Proof Brick Store.

| MOER. | BARTLETT. | NUCKOLLS. |

# S. H. MOER & CO.

Manufacturers and Dealers in

# LUMBER, TIMBER

## LATH AND SHINGLES.

A good Stock always on hand.

# CONTRACTORS AND BUILDERS,

### ORDERS SOLICITED.

**OFFICE ON FIFTH STREET, WEST DENVER.**

---

# HOWARD'S
# Jewelry Establishment

NORTH-EAST CORNER
**LARIMER and F STS.,**
DENVER CITY.

## WATCHES
AND
# JEWELRY

Neatly Repaired and Warranted.

**WATCH GLASSES, HANDS AND KEYS**

Accurately Fitted.

R. E. WHITSITT.     T. G. WILDMAN.

## WHITSITT & WILDMAN,

# REAL ESTATE AGENTS,

### BUY, SELL AND EXCHANGE

# LOTS AND LAND,

### RECORDER'S OFFICE,

Larimer Street,     DENVER CITY.

---

J. H. DUDLEY.     R. FULLERTON.

## J. H. DUDLEY & CO.

# CONVEYANCERS,

## NOTARIES PUBLIC,

And General Dealers in

# REAL ESTATE,

### LARIMER STREET,

BETWEEN F AND G.     DENVER CITY.

GEO. LYMAN MOODY.   CHAS. PHILIP MARION.

## MOODY & MARION,

### Civil Engineers and Architects,

OFFICE CORNER FIFTH AND CHERRY STS.,

WEST DIVISION.   DENVER CITY.

Surveying and Leveling done; Maps and Profiles promptly executed; Designs made for Buildings, Bridges, etc., etc.

---

A. C. HUNT.   JOHN M. CLARK.   A. SAGENDORF.

## A. C. HUNT & CO.

## REAL ESTATE

—AND—

## GENERAL BUSINESS AGENTS,

Fifth Street, near Ferry, Denver.

J. M. CLARK is a Civil Engineer and Surveyor.

---

## WM. LARIMER, Jr.

## REAL ESTATE AGENT.

## HOUSES, LOTS AND LANDS

### FOR SALE.

Larimer Street,   DENVER CITY.

---

## J. J. SAVILLE, M. D.

## Physician and Surgeon,

### DENVER CITY.

# CHICAGO BAKERY,
### BLAKE STREET,
**FRED. MARK, - - - PROPRIETOR.**

## FRESH BREAD, PIES, CAKES, ETC.
### To be had at all times.

## RESIDENCE AND BUSINESS LOTS.

The undersigned offers for sale in West Denver, upwards of one hundred RESIDENCE AND BUSINESS LOTS, centrally located; also, two good BUSINESS LOTS; also, one FULL BLOCK, about one mile from corner of Sixth and Ferry Streets, containing three acres; as it adjoins the Platte River, it is well adapted for a handsome residence or garden.

WM. RUTHERFORD.

Apply to J. B. DOYLE & CO.

## W. E. CARTER,
# GENERAL MERCHANT,
### WHOLESALE DEALER IN
## SHIRTS, DRAWERS, HOSIERY, ETC.
### 69 Main Street, St. Louis, Mo.

## W. E. CARTER,
**Larimer Street,**      **DENVER CITY.**

## ROCKY MOUNTAIN BREWERY.

### ALWAYS ON HAND, A GOOD SUPPLY OF
# LAGER BEER AND ALE,
### AT THEIR BREWERY.

**SOLOMON & CO., Denver.**

*Orders left with J. B. DOYLE & CO., will receive prompt attention.*

## HAAS & BRO.

### BRANCH STORE FROM LEAVENWORTH CITY,

DEALERS IN

Cigars, Meerschaum Pipes,

## SNUFF AND PLAYING CARDS,

Corner F and Larimer Sts.

DENVER CITY.

---

IRAM NYE.  BEN. F. BRADLEY.  WINCHESTER HALL.

## NYE, BRADLEY & CO.,

Wholesale and Retail Dealers in

## HARDWARE, CUTLERY,

### IRON, STEEL, NAILS, ETC.

ALSO, DEALERS IN

### RUBBER BELTING, PACKING, HOSE, GAS PIPE,

Copper, Mill and Circular Saws, Force and Suction Pumps,

### BAR IRON, NAIL ROD, HORSE SHOES, HORSE NAILS, ETC.

We have also a large and full assortment of

### MINERS' AND MACHINISTS' SUPPLIES,

Building Hardware, Agricultural Implements, etc., etc.

**Blake Street,**  DENVER, J. T.

# NEW YORK STORE.

## STETTAUER & BRO.

DEALERS IN

# DRY GOODS, CLOTHING,

Notions, Boots and Shoes, etc.

**Larimer Street,**          DENVER CITY.

Nos. 55½ and 57 Delaware Street, Leavenworth; No. 63 Barclay Street, New York.

## DENVER VINEGAR FACTORY.

**HENRY SCHWENK, Proprietor,**

DEALER IN ALL KINDS OF

# LIQUORS, WINES AND CIGARS,

LARIMER STREET,

BETWEEN F AND G STREETS,        DENVER CITY.

## GOLDEN CITY

is fifteen miles from Denver, situated on Clear creek, one mile from where the latter stream leaves the mountain canon. It is situated in a beautiful valley, surrounded by a large range of mountains.

Golden City has several extensive business houses, hotels, etc. Population, about 500, and rapidly increasing.

### BUSINESS DIRECTORY.

West, Blunt & Co., Miners supplies.
Davidson, Breath & Co., Clothiers.
JOHN M. FERREL, Miner's Hotel.
O. B. Harvey, Jefferson House.
W. H. Gauson, Idaho House.
G. N. Belcher, Elkhorn House.
John F. Kirby, Attorney at Law.
I. E. Hardy, M. D.
C. C. Carpenter, Saloon.
Crow & Brundy, Bowling Saloon.
James McDonald, Real Estate.
Burt & Berthoud, Eng'rs and Surv'rs
R. R. Davis, Real Estate.
West, Blunt & Co., Blacksmiths.
Michael Pott, Butcher.
W. A. H. Loveland, News Dealer.

# MINER'S HOTEL,

## JOHN M. FERREL, - - PROPRIETOR.

### FIRST STREET,

### GOLDEN CITY, □ □ □ JEFFERSON.

## MOUNT VERNON

is situated on the Denver, Mt. Vernon and Gregory Toll road, at the entrance of the canon, where the road enters the mountains, fifteen miles from Denver. It has a population of about 200. Lime, and the crude material for making Plaster of Paris, is found in great abundance; the finest of stone for building purposes, having the appearance of common marble, is obtained here in inexhaustible quantities.

---

# DENVER CITY, MT. VERNON
— AND —
# GREGORY

# TOLL ROAD.

THIS IS THE

## SHORTEST, BEST AND MOST TRAVELED ROAD
### TO ALL PARTS OF THE MINES.

The Roads are always kept in good repair, and

## TOLL CHEAPER THAN BY ANY OTHER ROAD.

### OFFICERS OF ROAD.

GOV. STEELE, Pres.          J. C. NELSON, Vice-Pres.
JAMES GALBRETH, Secretary.

---

# MOUNT VERNON HOUSE,

### Mount Vernon, Rocky Mountains.

G. MORRISON, - - - PROPRIETOR.

This House is now ready for the reception of guests, and the patronage of the Traveling public is respectfully solicited.

## GOLDEN GATE,

situated two miles North-West from Golden City, contains a few Business Houses, Hotels, etc.

## MOUNTAIN CITY BUSINESS DIRECTORY.

Smith, Parmelee & Co., Supplies.
W. H. Bates & Co., Groceries.
Dr. Headley, Physician.
William Cook, Blacksmith.
Dr. Ellis, Druggist.
A. K. Philleo, Druggist.
Warner & Smith, Groceries.
Charles Taescher, Restaurant.
Kline & Trappe, Restaurant.
E. R. Young, Boots and Shoes.
William Quigley, Tinsmith.
N. P. Simpson, Tailor.
Levi Beauchamp, Daguerreotypes.
Dr. J. H. Day, Chemist.

Brown & Cowan, Com. Merchants.
Theatre, M'lle Haydee & Co.
Waterman & Morris, Restaurant.
H. T. Cruse, Restaurant,
Colman & Weil, Saloon and Bakery.
R. B. Smock, Smock's Hotel.
H. Ferris, Ferris' House.
H. Cooper, Gregory House.
McLain, Gray & Smith, Att. at Law
Post & Mason, Attorneys at Law.
Truman & Co., Butchers.
John Clark, Jeweler.
E. Burgen, Gunsmith.

## EUREKA GULCH.

Names and occupation of Business and Professional men in Eureka Gulch.

James Bingley, Butcher.
D. B. Davis, Boarding House.

Cornell & Bro., General Assortment.
Myron Andrews, " "

Thatcher, Ralstein & Co., Clothing and Provisions.

## CENTRAL CITY

is 35 miles from Denver, and is situated at the junction of Spring, Nevada and Eureka Gulches. In May last, the first frame building was erected—now it boasts of a population of about 500, which is rapidly increasing. Some of the most extensive establishments in the mountains are located here. Its natural position, with the rapid developement of the mining region immediately surrounding, places her in the front rank of mountain cities.

The following are the names of the principal business houses and professional men in the city:

JACOBS & CO., Miner's Supplies.
J. B. Henry, Miner's Supplies.
J. W. Smith, Physician.
WM. RUTHERFORD. See adv. General Assortment.
H. F. Kingsman, Saloon and Bakery
Rowth & Cannon, Bakery.
W. C. Simpson, Central City House.
Fox's News Depot.
GOODWIN, HARPER & STANLEY Restaurant. See adv.
GEO. CORRYELL, M. D. See adv
Lewis Berry, Pawnbroker.
R. B. Smock, Hotel.
H. Griel, Washing and Ironing.
J. H. HENSE, Watches. See adv.
Block & Barnard, Butchers.
A. W. Hall, Central Hall.
New York Hotel, E. C. Sparks.
F. M. DENNY, M. D. See adv.

J. J. Moore, Lawyer.
H. G. Otis, Merchandise.
Lewis Hamilton, Groceries.
Stettauer & Co., Dry Goods.
Dr. W. T. Ellis, Druggist.
J. B. Heckman, U. S. Post Master.
MORSE & McCOOK, Att'ys at Law
REESE & KRATZER, Watches.
Charles Hopping, Daguerreotypes.
Thos. Smith, Recorder Eureka Dist.
L. B. Wellman, Rec. Spring Gulch.
Chas. Lesmoineaux, French Bakery
F. Tobin, Clothing, Books, Varieties
John Armor, General Assortment.
NUCKOLLS & HAWKE, Dry Goods
Tibbits & Snider, Restaurant.
H. P. Coolidge, Stoves and Tinware
William Sloan, Livery Stable.
D. C. Corbin, Dupont's Powder.
BELA S. BUELL, News Depot.

## BOOK STORE AND NEWS DEPOT.

### BELA S. BUELL,

DEALER IN

### Books, Stationery, Wall Paper

NEWSPAPERS AND PERIODICALS.

CIGARS AND TOBACCO,

CENTRAL CITY, ROCKY MOUNTAINS.

# O. K. STORE.

## JACOBS & CO.,
Wholesale and Retail Dealers in

# GROCERIES,
## PROVISIONS,
—AND—
# OUTFITTING,
### CENTRAL CITY.

---

## JOHN H. HENSE,
### DEALER IN
# WATCHES,
## CLOCKS
AND
# JEWELRY

### CENTRAL CITY.

Watches, Clocks and Jewelry repaired and warranted, or money refunded.

Jewelry of all kinds made to order on the shortest notice.

## WM. RUTHERFORD,
## DRY GOODS JOBBER,
### GROCERIES, HARDWARE
—AND—
## COMMISSION MERCHANT
### CENTRAL CITY.
☛ GOLD AND SILVER CLAIMS FOR SALE.

---

### CENTRAL CITY
## SALOON AND RESTAURANT,

No pains have been spared to make this a First Class House. The tables are at all times supplied with the best the market and the season affords, while the bar is stored with the choicest Wines, Liquors and Cigars.

Connected with the establishment is a Restaurant, Where MEALS, BOARD and REFRESHMENTS can be had at all hours.

**GOODWIN, HARPER & STANLEY.**

---

J. H. REESE. : : : : : : : F. W. KRATZER.
### REESE & KRATZER,
## SILVERSMITHS
—AND—
### JEWELERS,
CENTRAL CITY, ROCKY MOUNTAINS.

---

HARLEY B. MORSE.                    EDWARD M. McCOOK.
### MORSE & M'COOK,
## ATTORNEYS AT LAW,
CENTRAL CITY, ROCKY MOUNTAINS.

**Practice in all the Courts of the Territory.**

## NUCKOLLS & HAWKE,
Wholesale and Retail Dealers in

# DRY GOODS

## HARDWARE,
### HATS, CAPS, BOOTS, SHOES, CLOTHING, DRUGS
PAINTS, OILS, GLASS AND CHINA WARE, IRON,
NAILS, CASTINGS, STOVES AND TINWARE,
SHEET IRON AND CUTLERY,

## FLOUR, BACON, LARD
—AND—
### Miners' Goods Generally,
### CENTRAL CITY.

### A GOOD ASSORTMENT OF CHOICE LIQUORS.

FRANKLIN M. DENNY,

## PHYSICIAN AND SURGEON

CENTRAL CITY,

ROCKY MOUNTAINS.

DR. GEORGE CORRYELL,

## Physician and Surgeon

CENTRAL CITY.

OFFICE—on East side of Spring and Nevada Gulches, above the United States Post Office.

## NEVADA CITY,

In Nevada Gulch, is situated in the centre of the best quartz mining gulches in the Rocky Mountains. It has a large number of business houses. Its population is spread over an area of about three miles. Population about 8,000.

The following are the names of the principal business and professional men in the city:

Lightner, Street & Co., Groceries.
C. Anderson, Jewelry.
Adams & Russel, Store.
Mills & Debord, Groceries.
Fred. Wezstein, Butcher.
Hugh Gamble, Saloon and Groceries.
Van Deren & Co., Groceries.
IDAHO HALL and THEATER, S. B. Holly.
J. M. Kissan, Groceries.
Judge Jones, Idaho Hall.
R. D. Darlington, Rec. Nevada Dist.
Wm. Kimberland, Attorney at Law.
F. Mayer, Dry Goods.
Dr. A. Phinney, General Assortment.
J. D. Murphy, Provisions, Clothing.

S. M. HALL, Bakery and Saloon.
J. H. Norton, General Assortment.
K. D. Shugart, Bakery.
Isaac Armitage & Son, Blacksmiths.
Vinnedge, Taber & Co., Blacksmiths.
Krug & Bitzenhofer, Restaurant and Bakery.
W. H. Grafton, M. D.
Muir & Gest, Attorneys at Law.
C. Thompson, Attorney at Law.
Bradford & Randall, Att'ys at Law.
Chas. Alber, Butcher.
J. J. Pratt, Engineer and Surveyor.
F. T. Sherman, Assay Office.
Emil Housding, Painter.

## IDAHO HALL,

### NEVADA CITY,

### S. B. HOLLY, - - Proprietor.

THIS IS THE

### ONLY PUBLIC HALL IN NEVADA.

Court House and Theater in this Building.

### THE IDAHO SALOON

Is always supplied with a choice assortment of

**PURE LIQUORS AND BEST HAVANA CIGARS.**

# NEVADA HOUSE,
## NEVADA CITY,
S. M. HALL, - - - - Proprietor.

In connection with the above House, we have a

## BAKERY AND FIRST-CLASS RESTAURANT,
Where Meals can at all times be had.

---

### SPRINGFIELD CITY.

is situated in Spring Gulch, between Missouri and Central City. Population, about 200.

The following are the names of the principal business and professional men in the city:

Albert Barber, Groceries, etc.
Starr & Johnson, Groceries, etc.
EVANS & STOKES, Groceries and Provisions. See adv.
Aug. Hommel, Vinegar Factory.

Thos. Barnes, Billiard Saloon.
Tompklinson & Bro., Butchers.
Mark Allen, Merchant.
Pleas, Byers & Robinson, Groceries and Provisions.

---

# EVANS & STOKES,
### DEALERS IN
## GROCERIES AND PROVISIONS,
### BOOTS, SHOES, CLOTHING, DRY GOODS
### AND MINERS' TOOLS.

SPRINGFIELD CITY, - - - ROCKY MOUNTAINS.

---

### MISSOURI CITY.

The following are the names of the principal business houses and professional men in Missouri City:

Curran & Mead, General Assortm't.
Baxter & Butler, Butchers.
Chas. Warga, Butcher.
John Taffa, Tailor.
Ed. L. Nash, Baker.
Buchanan & Co., Saloon.
A. H. Jones, Saloon.

James Clarkson, Blacksmith.
J. H. Haines, Groceries.
A. Amburgh, Merchant.
W. C. Asher, Physician.
Consolidated Ditch Co., Green Russell, Pres.; A. H. Owens, Sec.

## BORTONSBURGH.

One mile west of Missouri City, in the centre of a rich quartz mining region the above named town is situated. Population, about 200.

L. W. Borton, Attorney at Law.
Borton & Kerr, Groceries and Provisions.

---

## L. W. BORTON,
## ATTORNEY AT LAW
### AND NOTARY PUBLIC.

Will practice before the different Miners' Courts, and attend promptly to the collection of debts.

**BORTONSBURGH, - - - - ROCKY MOUNTAINS.**

---

Names of business houses and professional men in Missouri and Russell's Districts:

J. FRANK COOPER, Attorney at Law. See adv.

| | |
|---|---|
| E. Norton & Co., Groceries. | C. S. Fassett, Rec. Russell's Dist. |
| J. B. Richardson, Bakery. | Chris. Haack, Boot and Shoemaker. |
| Benson & Bro., Merchants. | Uhlman & Lange, Bakers. |

---

## J. FRANK COOPER,
## Attorney & Counselor at Law

**RUSSELL'S GULCH, Rocky Mountains.**

☞ Practices in all the Courts of the Territory.

## COLORADO CITY,

El Paso county, is situated about 90 miles south of Denver. The location of the city is a good one; several soda, sulphur and other springs in the immediate neighborhood. The following are the names of the business men in the city:

Tappan & Co., General Assortment. | Dunn & Co., Grocers.
Loeb & Co., Liquors.

## BRECKINRIDGE

is about 9 miles north-west of Tarryall City, on the road to the Blue River Diggings. Population, about 200. The following are the names of the business men:

Shalcapf & Whitney, Merchants. | Hall & Co., Saloon.
Rice & Co., Merchants. | — Myers, Bakery.
— Cook, Hotel. | C. P. Hall, Recorder.
G. Bissell, Judge of District Court.

## HAMILTON.

A place of about 200 inhabitants, has got several business houses, hotels, etc. Situated about 2 miles north-west of Tarryall City.

## ST. JOSEPH, MO.

From here there is a choice of two ferries, to cross the Missouri River, viz: the St. Joseph and Ellwood Ferry, which lands you on the opposite side of the river from St. Joseph; and the St. Joseph and Bellmont Ferry Company, which lands you up the Missouri River four miles above St. Joseph. The prices of ferriage on both boats are the same. From either Ellwood or Bellmont the road goes through a thickly settled country, until you reach Kinnekuk, 38 miles from St. Joseph—here you strike the Military Road to Fort Kearney. For table of distances, see Leavenworth route.

## WHAT IS NECESSARY FOR AN OUTFIT.

The following table comprises the "necessaries" for a trip across the plains. There are a great many other articles that could be enumerated under the head of "luxuries," which we do not deem necessary to publish. The following is intended for a six months' outfit for four men.

| | |
|---|---|
| 3 yoke of Oxen @ $75,...$225,00 | 1 Skillet,................$ 1,50 |
| 1 Wagon and Cover,........ 100,00 | 8 pairs Blankets,............ 24,00 |
| 3 Yokes and 3 Chains,..... 18,00 | 4 Water Buckets,............ 1,00 |
| 1 Whip,..................... 1,00 | 2 small Tin Buckets,....... 1,25 |
| 1 Tent,...................... 15,00 | 75 feet of Rope,............. 2,00 |
| 10 sacks Flour,............. 30,00 | 6 Table Spoons,............. 40 |
| 500 lbs Bacon,.............. 50,00 | 1 Camp Kettle,............... 1,25 |
| 80 lbs Coffee,............... 12,00 | 8 Sheets Iron, Long Tom, 5,00 |
| 80 lbs Star Candles,........ 7,00 | 4 Gold Pans,................. 3,00 |
| 10 lbs Tea,................... 5,00 | 4 Picks,...................... 4,00 |
| Yeast Powders,............ 4,00 | 4 Shovels,................... 5,00 |
| 80 lbs Salt,.................. 1,50 | 3 Axes,....................... 8,00 |
| 5 lbs Pepper,................ 1,00 | 2 Bread Pans,............... 75 |
| 4 bushels Beans,............ 8,00 | 1 Wagon Bucket,............ 1,00 |
| 10 gals. Vinegar,........... 8,00 | Hand Saw and Drawing |
| 25 lbs Bar Soap,............ 2,00 | Knife,...................... 3,00 |
| 25 lbs Gunpowder,......... 7,50 | 2 Chisels and Augers,..... 8,00 |
| 100 lbs Lead,................ 10,00 | 1 Dutch Oven for baking |
| Gun Caps, waterproof,.. 1,25 | Bread,...................... 1,25 |
| 1 gross Matches,............ 1,00 | 1 pair Gold Scales,......... 1,50 |
| 1 ten gal. Water keg,...... 1,25 | 1 twelve inch File,......... 40 |
| 1 Coffee Mill,............... 75 | 1 Shingling Hatchet,....... 75 |
| 2 Coffee Pots,............... 1,50 | 1 Crowbar,.................. 1,50 |
| 8 Tin Plates,................ 50 | 2 Gimlets,................... 15 |
| 8 Tin Cups,.................. 50 | 10 yds. Cotton Drilling,.... 1,20 |
| 2 Frying Pans,.............. 1,50 | 10 lbs Cut and Wro't Nails 85 |
| 4 Butcher Knives,.......... 2,50 | 1 Whetstone,................ 20 |
| 12 Knives and Forks,...... 1,50 | |

For Tents, see advertisement of Gilbert, Hubbard & Co.
For Hardware, see advertisement of Larrabee & North.
For Guns, Pistols and Firearms, see advertisement of Chas. A. Eaton.

## DIFFERENT KINDS OF QUARTZ MILLS.

It would be an impossibility, in this work, to speak from experience, or with confidence, of the merits of the various quartz crushers, amalgamators, rastras, etc., with their several constructions. Each mill has its ardent advocate, and each owner or patentee claims peculiar advantages over all others. There will be a large number of mills brought before the public the ensuing spring, and it will remain for those interested to give them a careful examination. Among the most prominent of those that are now being introduced, we would call attention to the "Badger State," a new stamping mill, patented by Elmes & Bickford, Depere, Wis.; Higgins, Mowry & Co., 205 Randolph street, Chicago, have them for sale and for inspection. The "Chilian" mill, patented by W. H. & I. Scoville, and manufactured by C. Reissig & Co., Chicago, claims advantages as a pulverizer, crusher and amalgamator; see advertisement. The most prominent among those who have manufactured quartz mills for Pike's Peak, are Gates & Co., Chicago, Ill.; R. C. Totten & Co. and Gaty, McCune & Co.' St. Louis, Mo. There are numerous other makers in various portions of the country, whose names and addresses can be obtained by referring to our table containing statistics of quartz mills.

## LEAVENWORTH CITY, KANSAS.

We give below a table of distances from Leavenworth to Fort Kearney, via South Platte. The Leavenworth Road is followed until reaching Fort Leavenworth—from here the Military Road is followed. Streams all bridged. Farms and heavy settlements until you reach

|  | MILES. |
|---|---|
| LANCASTER—Wood, water and grass, | 30 |
| HURON—Wood, water and grass, | 13 |
| KINNEKUK—Small town, | 10 |
| WALUT CREEK, | 8 |
| LOCKLAND'S, | 13 |
| MINEHAH, | 18 |
| ASH POINT—good camping ground, | 12 |
| BLACK VERMILLION—good camping ground, | 12 |
| ELM CREEK—good camping ground, | 10 |
| BIG BLUE—Marysville settlement, stores, etc.—banks wide, swift current, 130 feet wide, | 14 |
| COTTONWOOD RANCHE—good camping ground, | 12 |
| ROCK CREEK—good camping ground. | 20 |
| LITTLE SANDY—road crosses ridge and then descends into Little Sandy, for grazing, | 14 |
| BIG SANDY—good camping ground, 200 feet wide, | 5 |
| CREEK—small stream flowing into Little Blue, | 8 |
| LITTLE BLUE RIVER—good camping ground, | 9 |
| Leave LITTLE BLUE—good wood, water and grass, | 44 |
| THIRTY-TWO MILE CREEK—wood, water and grass, | 8 |
| SAND HILL POND—some wood, no water or grass, | 14 |
| PLATTE RIVER—good grass, no wood, | 8 |
| FORT KEARNEY, | 12 |

## ATCHISON.

From here there is a large emigration starts yearly for the Gold Regions. A great many of the heavy freighters make this their depot and starting point. As the route from here is the same as from Leavenworth, we deem it unnecessary to make a repettition of distance. Five miles south-west of Atchison, you strike the Military Road. For further particulars, see route from Leavenworth.

## PLATTSMOUTH.

Names of Ranche Keepers and Distances to Ft. Kearney, commencing at

| | | | |
|---|---|---|---|
| Salt Creek, | 30 | miles to | Springs. |
| Blair's Ranche, | 4 | " | Well water. |
| Garfield's Ranche, | 6 | " | Scull Creek. |
| Simpson's " | 4 | " | Bone Creek, |
| Shinn's Ferry, Ranche, | 4 | " | Platte River, |
| Simpson's " | 12 | " | Big Spring. |
| Becroft & Newell's Ranche, | 7 | " | Clear Creek. |
| Carter's Ranche, | 5 | " | good well and river. |
| Nevin's " | 14 | " | " " " |
| Brackett's, | 15 | " | Old Pawnee Village—Platte. |
| Harmar & Biggs' Ranche, | 25 | " | well and Platte river. |
| Bissell & Earl's " | 15 | " | " " " |
| Mabin's Ranche, | 15 | " | Spring Creek. |
| Gregory & Graham's Ranche, | 15 | " | Junction St. Joseph road. |
| Fort Kearney, | 10 | " | |

Total distance, ............ 181 miles.

## SILVER MINES.

In the body of the book will be found an article treating on this subject. There have been attempts made by various assayists to give its proper value; but for want of proper specimens, or correct knowledge on the part of those that made the attempt, we do not deem it necessary to publish their assays. Their assays vary from fifty dollars to fifteen hundred dollars to the ton of ore. The supply of ore is inexhaustible, if future assays prove more satisfactory, and it becomes a verified fact, that it will pay to work and invest capital in the silver mines, the Fall River mines, together with the Quadary and Dirigo lodes of the Blue River, will become as familiar to the world as the celebrated "*Washoe*," of New Mexico.

## AMOUNT OF GOLD TAKEN FROM PIKE'S PEAK GOLD REGIONS.

Upon this subject, the opinions of those who are supposed to be posted, varies. As there is no specific way of arriving at a positive conclusion, we will have to give our readers the estimate that we obtained from various sources, leaving them to surmise as to its correctness.

Mr. A. D. Richardson, (special Pike's Peak Correspondent of the Boston *Journal*), a gentlemen who has paid particular attention to this subject, gives the yield of 1860 at five million dollars. From statistics taken in the fall of 1859, it was estimated that the yield was one million dollars; thus making the grand aggregate of six million dollars. When we take into consideration the want of confidence and capital, the inefficiency of machinery, and the deficiency of a practical knowledge on the part of a large proportion of those engaged in mining, we must certainly acknowledge the above figures to augur a bright future for the new Eldorado.

## MONTANA DISTRICT.

This is the name of a new District that has just been organized. Specimens of gold bearing quartz, taken from the Excelsior and Bourke lode, show indications of future rich discoveries. The gold can be seen through the specimens of quartz just shown us. It is situated about four miles north-west of the Half-Way House, on the Golden Gate and Gregory road.

## A. D. RICHARDSON, Esq.

We are happy to learn that this popular lecturer, is drawing crowded houses wherever he makes his appearance. As his subject, "*Pike's Peak,*" is one that the whole west takes an interest in, we commend him to the various Lyceums and Literary Associations throughout the west.

All communications should be addressed, 15 Cornhill, Boston, Mass.

### READ THE FOLLOWING NOTICES.

"LECTURE ON THE GOLD REGIONS.—We learn that A. D. Richardson, Esq., the well known correspondent of the Eastern Press, is to lecture in the States during the coming winter, repeating his popular discourse known as "Out West," and giving a new one entitled "Pike's Peak." Mr. Richardson is thoroughly familiar with this region, having first visited it in company with Horace Greeley, soon after the earliest discovery of the paying diggings, in June, 1859, and spent much of the time since in traveling through it. Our readers will remember that he was of the party which lately ascended Pike's Peak, and which succeeded, in spite of many hardships, in safely conducting up the first ladies who set foot upon the summit. He is a peculiarly graphic descriptive writer, as his letters to the New York *Tribune* and Boston *Journal* have long attested, and was eminently successful as a lecturer before Lyceums and other Literary Associatons in New England last winter. Our friends who may desire his services in the lecture field, should address him at 15 Cornhill, Boston.— *Daily Rocky Mountain News, Oct.* 9, 1860.

THE ROCKY MOUNTAIN GOLD REGION.—The third lecture before the Haverhill Library Association, was given to a crowded house on Friday evening, by A. D. Richardson, Esq.; subject, "Pike's Peak." The speaker described the wild life of the trappers who once roamed among the Rocky Mountains, as detailed to him by Kit Carson, and related his own experience and observations at Pike's Peak—some of them exceedingly amusing —during a visit, soon after the first paying discoveries. The audience was then taken in fancy upon a flying trip to that region now, to witness the wonderful changes of two years. The incidents of a journey with horses 665 miles across the plains; camp life; the prairie fire; the strange mirage of the desert; the appearance of Denver, (now a well built metropolis of 6,000 people) and the splendors of the mountain scenery, spread out like a panorama before that young city, were depicted with great vividness. The scenes in the diggings, operations in both quartz and gulch mining, and many incidents of life and society were next described, followed by a spirited account of a perilous journey up Pike's Peak, 14,500 feet above the sea level, by a party including two New England ladies, the first women who ever set foot upon the summit of that mountain. The view from the top is one of the finest on the American continent, and was graphically portrayed. The gold yield of 1860 was given as about five million dollars. The lecture was listened to with close attention, and was warmly applauded.—*Boston Daily Journal, Jan.* 1, 1861.

## OMAHA.

Omaha, Nebraska Territory, is situated on the west side of the Missouri River, about twenty miles above where the Platte empties into the Missouri. It is eminently designed as a great outfitting point. Steamboats ply between here and St. Joseph, running in connection with the Hannibal and St. Joseph Railroad; thus bringing her in direct connection with the East, A railroad will soon be completed between Chicago and Council Bluffs, and rapid progress is being made with the St. Joseph and Council Bluffs Railroad, thus giving Omaha superior railroad and river facilities.

From Omaha the road to Fort Kearney is thickly settled with thrifty farmers. Hay, corn and provisions can be purchased on the road at reasonable prices.

The following are the advertisements of the most responsible Banking and Outfitting Houses and general business men of the city; they have made extensive arrangements in order to meet the demands of the spring emigration.

---

# KOUNTZE BROTHERS,
# BANKERS,
### AND DEALERS IN
# GOLD DUST,
## OMAHA, NEBRASKA.

---

We buy Gold Dust at the highest market rates—or, if desired, send to the Mint on commission—paying nearly its value in cash when left with them, and remitting by draft for the balance due, together with the assay certificate, to any part of the United States, after they receive returns from the Mint.

Receive money on deposit and pay checks against the same.

Buy and sell Exchange, Coin and Bank Notes.

Make Collections throughout all parts of the United States, less only the current rate of exchange and actual expenses incurred.

### REFERENCES:

PARK BANK, New York; DREXEL & CO., Philadelphia; SPENCER, VILA & CO., Boston; JOHNSTON, BRO'S & CO., Baltimore; GILMORE, DUNLAP & CO., Cincinnati; ALLEN, COPP & NISBETT, St. Louis; HON. J. H. WOODWORTH, Ex-M. C., Chicago; WM. N. BYERS, Denver; THE MERCHANTS of Omaha.

## BARROWS, MILLARD & CO.,

# BANKERS

### AND DEALERS IN

# GOLD DUST

—AND—

# EXCHANGE,

### OMAHA, NEBRASKA.

---

We will pay the highest price in cash for Gold Dust; or, if desired, receive the same on commission, advancing seven-eighths of its value, and the balance on the return of the assay receipt, payable at the counter, or in New York Exchange, sent to any part of the United States. A small commission only, will be charged for attending to the business.

---

## BANK BUILDING,
### Farnham Street, South Side

---

### REFER TO

| | |
|---|---|
| TURNER & HOBBS, | Denver, J. T. |
| WOOLWORTH & MOFFATT, | " |
| STATE SAVINGS ASSOCIATION, | St. Louis, Mo. |
| GILMAN, SON & CO,. | New York. |
| SWEENY, RITTENHOUSE, FAUT & CO., | Washington, D. C. |

And all the Business Men in this section.

## GRAVES' GENERAL AGENCY
—AND—
# NEWS DEPOT,

Give place to fair Nebraska! To her towns of wealth and lore!
And to OMAHA, her Capitol—"Gem City of the West"—
Where the gold from modern Ophir is exchanged for other store.
Here GRAVES receives subscriptions, and of reading sells the best.

### The LATEST NEWS and CHOICEST LITERATURE
#### ALWAYS ON HAND.

ORDERS from the COUNTRY for any article of *Stationery, News, Literature or Art*, promptly attended to.

SUBSCRIPTIONS RECEIVED, single or in clubs, for all Papers and Publications, either in this country or in Europe.

Address, BYRON P. GRAVES,
OMAHA, Nebraska Ter.

☞ Book-Binding neatly and durably done in every style.

## THE LARGEST CLOTHING HOUSE IN OMAHA!

### M. HELLMAN & CO.,
Wholesale and Retail Dealers in

# READY-MADE CLOTHING
—AND—
### GENTS' FURNISHING GOODS,

FARNHAM STREET, next door to the cor. of Thirteenth,

OMAHA, N. T.

## CASH PAID FOR HIDES AND FURS.
### Gold Dust taken in exchange for Clothing.

## HURFORD & BROTHER,

Wholesale and Retail Dealers in

# HARDWARE

AGRICULTURAL IMPLEMENTS,

## LUMBER
AND
## BUILDING MATERIALS.

We have the largest Stock of Goods in our line north of St. Louis, and offer particular inducements to EMIGRANTS going to the

## GOLD MINES

in the way of Implements and general HARDWARE adapted for the Miner's use. They have kept an AGENT in the Mines for the past year especially for the purpose of ascertaining

## THE EXACT ARTICLE WANTED

in the way of TOOLS for

## SUCCESSFUL GOLD MINING

We cordially invite an examination of our large stock of Goods.

Our Store is situated on

## DOUGLAS STREET,
JUST ABOVE THE POST OFFICE,

**OMAHA, N. T.**

BUY YOUR GOODS AT THE CHEAP CASH STORE
—OF—
M'GEATH, BROTHER & CO.,
WHOLESALE AND RETAIL DEALERS IN
Foreign and Domestic Dry Goods,
CLOTHING,
GROCERIES,
HARDWARE,
BOOTS AND SHOES, ETC.
FARNHAM STREET
Between Thirteenth and Fourteenth Streets, South Side,
OMAHA, N. T.

J. H. LACEY.                              JOHN McCORMICK.
LACEY & McCORMICK,
WHOLESALE GROCERS,
FARNHAM STREET,
OMAHA, ▫ ▫ ▫ ▫ NEBRASKA.

PUNDT & KOENIG,
DEALERS IN
GROCERIES AND PROVISIONS,
AT THE O K STORE,
OMAHA, - - - - - NEBRASKA.

# THOMAS L. SHAW,
## Watchmaker and Jeweler

FARNHAM STREET, OMAHA.

ALL KINDS OF MUSICAL INSTRUMENTS AND JEWELRY REPAIRED and warranted to give satisfaction.

PIKE'S PEAK GOLD RINGS MANUFACTURED TO ORDER. A CAREfully selected assortment of Clocks.

## KEITH'S HOTEL,

CORNER OF THIRTEENTH AND HARNEY STREETS,

OMAHA, N. T.

M. W. KEITH, Proprietor,

## The Loupe Fork Ferry Co.,
### AT COLUMBUS, N. T.,

Have their Ferry in PERFECT RUNNING ORDER. They have TWO LARGE BOATS, an accommodating and efficient agent, with plenty of help, and they will spare no effort to cross emigrants with comfort and without delay. This Route offers peculiar advantages to the emigrant over any other.

O. P. HURFORD, Secretary.

## OMAHA BREWERY

F. KRUG, PROPRIETOR,

FARNHAM STREET,

OMAHA,   -  -  -   NEBRASKA.

## ALEX. McAUSLAND & SON,
# GUNSMITHS
### AND MACHINISTS.

## IRON, BRASS AND WOOD TURNING
DONE WITH NEATNESS AND DISPATCH.

☞ NOTARIAL SEALS ENGRAVED AND SAFE LOCKS REPAIRED WITH CARE.

*WORKSHOP, CORNER FOURTEENTH AND DOUGLAS STS.,*
## OMAHA, N. T.

## A. J. SIMPSON,
# CARRIAGE AND WAGON
### MANUFACTORY,
DOUGLAS STREET, OPPOSITE TREMONT HOUSE,

## OMAHA, NEBRASKA.

☞ REPAIRING IN ALL ITS BRANCHES. ☜

# CENTRAL MEAT MARKET,
THIRTEENTH STREET, South of Post Office.

A GOOD ASSORTMENT OF
## DRIED AND OTHER MEATS
PUT UP EXPRESSLY FOR THOSE
### INTENDING TO VISIT THE GOLD MINES.
DALLOW & HYMAS, Omaha, Nebraska.

J. R. PORTER.  H. P. DEUEL.
## PORTER & DEUEL,
## Storage, Forwarding and Commission Merchants,
Steamboat and General Agents.    Agents for Valentines Freight Express Company.

## OMAHA CITY, ▫ ▫ ▫ ▫ NEBRASKA.

☞ Particular attention given to the sale of Bacon, Flour and all kinds of Merchandise. Liberal Cash advances made on Consignments.   ☞ Mark Goods care PORTER & DEUEL, Omaha City, N. T.

REFERENCES.—W. H. SHIPMAN & CO., St. Joseph; F. B. KERCHEVAL & CO., St. Joseph; BUDDEE & JACOBS, Denver City; JOS. McENTIRE, St. Louis; KOUNTZE BRO., Bankers, Omaha; BARROWS, MILLARD & Co., Bankers, Omaha; Merchants of Omaha and Officers of Missouri River Packets generally.

# HOMAN'S LIVERY STABLE

is prepared to Stable Horses and Cattle by the Day, Week or Month, for Miners and others.

## BLACKSMITHING AND WHEEL-WRIGHTING

DONE WITH DISPATCH.

**OMAHA, NEBRASKA.**

---

# FARMERS' HOME,

JOHN VERGES, - - - - PROPRIETOR,

Cor. Thirteenth and Farnham Streets,

Opposite the O K STORE.

**OMAHA, N. T.**

Recommends itself to the traveling public by the moderate prices that we charge. Good Stabling attached.

---

## D. C. SUTPHEN,

# Tobacconist and Confectioner,

WHOLESALE AND RETAIL DEALER IN

## C. BRONSON'S FINE CUT TOBACCO,

ALSO, MANUFACTURER OF

## ALL KINDS OF CANDY

AND DEALER IN FRESH FRUIT,

**OMAHA CITY, - - - - - NEBRASKA.**

---

# TREMONT HOUSE,

Opposite the Post Office,

**OMAHA CITY, - - - - NEBRASKA.**

W. F. SWEEZY, - - Proprietor.

## TABLE OF DISTANCES FROM KANSAS CITY TO DENVER,
### BY THE SOUTHERN OR ARKANSAS ROUTE.

It is an undisputed fact that Kansas City is the most preferable starting point for those intending to take the Arkansas route. This is by far the most preferable route for those intending to start before February or March, as the feed for stock on this route is generally about one month earlier than on any of the other routes. The road, generally speaking, is good, and from the amount of travel that annually passes over it, there is no danger to be apprehended from the Indians. From Kansas City to

| | MILES. |
|---|---|
| BULL CREEK—water and grass, | 20 |
| BLACK JACK—Willow Spring Settlement, | 6 |
| ELM CREEK—wood, water and grass, | 10 |
| COUNCIL GROVE, | 14 |
| DIAMOND SPRING—Santa Fe Mail Station, | 16 |
| LAST SPRING—good water and grass, | 16 |
| COTTONWOOD CREEK—Trading Post—wood, water and grass, | 20 |
| TURKEY CREEK—good grass and water, | 25 |
| LITTLE ARKANSAS—wood, water and grass—Trading Post, | 15 |
| COW CREEK, | 2 |
| FLUM BUTTES, | 12 |
| ARKANSAS—wood and water, | 18 |
| WALNUT CREEK—Allison's Ranche, | 5 |
| ASH CREEK—water not reliable, | 22 |
| PAWNEE FORK—wood and water, | 6 |
| COOK CREEK, | 33 |
| WHITEWATER—water scarce, | 20 |
| FORT ATKINSON, | 10 |
| Cross SANTA FE TRAIL, | 17 |

From here, for a distance of 150 miles, the country is very barren.

| | |
|---|---|
| BENT'S FORT—wood, water and grass, | 150 |
| BENT'S OLD FORT, | 40 |
| HUERFANO, | 40 |
| FONTAINE QUE BOUILLE, | 15 |
| CROSSING—plenty of water and grass, | 18 |
| JIM'S CAMP, | 16 |
| O'FALLEY'S GROVE, | 12 |
| BRUSH CORRALLE, | 13 |
| HEAD OF CHERRY CREEK, | 14 |
| DENVER, | 28 |

## SCOVILLE'S
# PATENT PREMIUM QUARTZ MILL,
### Being a Combined Crusher, Pulverizer and Amalgamator.

This Mill is unquestionably superior in every respect to any Stamp Mill. It pulverizes faster than the best Stamp, in proportion to the power applied, and all material passing through it is reduced to a *uniform* and *thorough fineness*, that cannot be obtained by any other style of machinery heretofore used. It is more durable and less liable to get out of order than Stamps, and uses far less water, besides being a complete and perfect Amalgamator in itself. For circulars, information, or further particulars, inquire of the manufacturers,

### C. REISSIG & CO.
Chicago Steam Boiler Works, Chicago, Ill.

Also, manufacture STEAM ENGINES and BOILERS, and all kinds of MACHINERY and CASTINGS.

## CHICAGO, ILLINOIS.

Emigrants and business men starting or passing through this City, on their way to the gold mines, will find it to their advantage to call at the establishments whose advertisements follow this notice. They have got especial claims upon the emigration, as their stocks are selected and especially adapted for the wants of the emigration.

## PIKE'S PEAK OUTFITTING.

**92 LAKE STREET.** } Opposite the Tremont House, { **92 LAKE STREET,**

### CHICAGO, ILLINOIS.

## CHAS. A. EATON,

IS PREPARED TO FURNISH

### COMPLETE OUTFITS FOR THE MINES,

—SUCH AS—

Tools of all kinds, Tents, Blankets, Rubber Goods,

**POWDER, SAFETY FUSE, PISTOLS AND OTHER WEAPONS,**

### GOLD SCALES, ETC.

Every effort will be made to furnish companies and individuals with everything necessary for the trip.

☞ Pike's Peak Directory and Guide to the Gold Mines for sale.

---

C. R. LARRABEE.                           ROB'T L. NORTH.

## LARRABEE & NORTH,

DEALERS IN

# HARDWARE,

Cutlery, Guns, Mill Saws, Files,

**TOOLS, BUILDERS' MATERIALS, ENGINEERING INSTRUMENTS, ETC., ETC.**

No. 174 Lake Street,

**CHICAGO,**    -   -   -   -    **ILLINOIS.**

## TENTS, WAGON COVERS AND TARPAULINS,

Of every description, on hand and made to order.

## GILBERT HUBBARD & CO.
# SHIP CHANDLERS
### AND SAIL MAKERS,

Nos. 205 and 207 South Water Street, corner of Wells,

## CHICAGO, ILLINOIS.

WHOLESALE AND RETAIL DEALERS IN

# TWINES AND CORDAGE,

Manilla and Tarred Rope, Sail Duck, Bags and Bagging, Wool, Seine and Gill-Net Twine, Nets and Seines, Oakum, Tar, Pitch, Paints, Oils, Chains, Anchors, Tackle Blocks,

**COAL TAR, ROOFING PITCH AND FELTING.**

# WM. D. BAKER,
## WOOD ENGRAVING.

Rooms, N. E. corner Clark and Randolph Sts.

## CHICAGO, □ □ □ ILLINOIS.

Views of Cities, Buildings, Machinery, Portraits, Lodge Seals, Maps, etc., etc., engraved in the best style, and at reasonable prices.

## TINTED BUSINESS ENVELOPES,
Engraved and Printed to order at New York Prices.

SATISFACTION GUARANTEED.
P. O. Box 2197.

## CHAS. SHOBER,
**FIRST PREMIUM**
## LITHOGRAPHER,
No. 109 Lake Street,

P. O. Box 4069.                                CHICAGO, ILL.

RECOMMENDS HIS ESTABLISHMENT FOR THE ENGRAVING OF

## BONDS, CERTIFICATES, NOTES,
### DRAFTS, CHECKS,
Business, Visiting and Address Cards, Letter-Heads, Bill-Heads,

LABELS, SHOW CARDS. PORTRAITS, VIEWS, PLANS, MAPS, ETC.

Which he prints in black or colors, in the best style.

## MOUNTING AND COLORING OF MAPS,
**RULING OF PAPER AND BINDING OF DRAFT BOOKS,**
Also done in best style, and promptly executed.

## ST. LOUIS ADVERTISEMENTS.

# IMPROVED
# QUARTZ MILL,
### Manufactured only at the WESTERN FOUNDRY,
### R. C. TOTTEN & CO., Proprietors, ST. LOUIS, MO.

## DESCRIPTION OF MILL.

**THE STAMPERS** are of any required number and are made in the ordinary way of wrought iron and cast iron combined, if parties prefer—but we *recommend* the **Solid wrought Iron Stamper**, to be the only one that combines *durability* and *efficiency* in the *highest degree*. The experience of all the 15 Mills, manufactured by us last spring, and now in *successful operation* at the Peak, proves the *superiority* of the Solid Wrought Iron Stamper, which we introduced and of which we were the only manufacturers. The difficulty with Stampers made in the usual way, is that the Wrought Iron and Cast Iron cannot be so fastened together—either by being *screwed* or *cast* together so as to prevent their becoming separated—sooner or later, by the constant *jarring* of the Stamper. A solid Stamper will last *Fifty Years*. The Stampers revolve as they are lifted.

THE COLLARS are a *solid part* of the Stamper, and there is no possibility of their working loose and giving trouble, which *must* be the case sooner or later with all Cast Iron Collars *screwed* or *cast* on the stem. Another advantage in our collars is that they do not wear away like the cast collars. It is a well known fact, that Cast Iron and Wrought Iron surface wear better together than Cast Iron and Cast Iron—our collars being *Wrought Iron* and the cam that lifts them *Cast Iron*, present surfaces that will not wear so fast as where the Collar and Cam are both Cast Iron, as in *all other* mills. A party owning one of our mills, writes: "Your Collars will last *fifty* years—ours are not worn a particle." We do not make our Collars *adjustable* for reasons given below.

THE FACES OR SHOES of the *Stampers* are movable and are made of Chilled Iron—chilled *six inches* deep, if preferred—but we recommend either a SOLID STEEL SHOE, with a *Wrought Iron stem*, or a Wrought Iron shoe faced with steel. THE SOLID STEEL FACES can be furnished almost as CHEAP as the CAST IRON. We have obtained, at considerable expense, a *secret* process, discovered in France, and used for *hardening* Mill Picks, for dressing Burr Mill Stones. By this process we can *harden* our steel faces so hard as to outwear ten set of chilled faces. This is a valuable discovery for mill men.

THE CAMS and CAM SHAFTS. The Cams are very durable and so made as to lift equally well from *fifteen to twenty* inches or more if desired. They are of such a shape as to do away with any necessity for an *adjustable Collar*, as they will *accommodate themselves* to the *wearing* of the shoe of the stamper and the *different quantities of material* in the boxes, *without any alteration or attention*. Adjustable Collars on the contrary, to do any good, would have to be moved every *ten* or *fifteen* minutes, and consequently are *never used* in practice at all, but will sooner or later give trouble by wearing loose. The Cams are so arranged on the shaft that the stampers in each box fall one at a time, which has been found in practice to be the *most effectual way*. The CAM SHAFTS are made of best Iron, and not less than *four* inches diameter, preventing any quivering or shaking. They work in Bearings of the most approved construction.

THE MORTAR BOXES, into which the quartz is thrown, having to stand the entire shock of all the Machinery—we will make much more *durable* than heretofore and perfectly *water tight*. We now have the benefit of two seasons in the construction of these mortars, and are determined to avail ourselves of the information we have obtained, and will make them without regard to expense. The GRATING will be so arranged as to be removed and replaced with *great dispatch* and still be *water tight*. The dies on which the stampers fall will be made of superior *Chilled Cast Iron*, or will be made of *Solid Cast Steel*, if parties desire it, at *same price*.

DRAWINGS, to enable parties to get out timber, and giving directions how to erect, will be furnished with every mill free of charge.

*Parties having friends at the Peak, can have them call upon the following mill owners, or any others using our mills. Communications, in relation to prices and terms, will receive prompt attention.*

### MILL OWNERS AT THE PEAK.

| | |
|---|---|
| GEO. C. COLEMAN, Eureka Gulch. | KENOSHA QUARTZ CO., Nevada Gulch. |
| RUSSEL & AVERY, Nevada do | DORN MINING CO., do do |
| J. A. HALE, Chase's Gulch. | W. E. BROWN & CO., Post Office, Mountain City. |
| HARRIS & WHEELER, Toll Gate Mill. | W. S. CANDEE, do do do do |

## COUNCIL BLUFFS, IOWA.

Is situated on the East side of the Missouri River. It possesses some of the finest buildings West of St. Louis. Two railroads, one from Chicago, and the other the Platte Country Railroad, being a continuation of the Hannibal and St. Joseph Railroad, will, when completed, make this their Western terminus. A large portion of last year's emigration passed through here.

The following Business Houses, Hotels, etc., have the best facilities for meeting the wants of the spring emigration.

## WILLIAM F. KITER,
# BOOK BINDER
### —AND—
## BLANK BOOK MANUFACTURER,
### COUNCIL BLUFFS, IOWA.

H. C. FREDRICKSON.     W. C. JACKSON.

## FREDRICKSON & JACKSON,
#### DEALERS IN
# OUTFITTING GOODS,
### DRY GOODS,
### GROCERIES, PROVISIONS AND GRAIN,
Lower Broadway, Council Bluffs.

## COUNCIL BLUFFS DISTILLERY.
### SILL & BOWEN,
# DISTILLERS AND RECTIFIERS
### PURE SPIRITS AND HIGHWINES
#### PUT UP ANY PROOF DESIRED.
### COUNCIL BLUFFS, IOWA.
McBRIDE & SILL, Agents.

## J. M. PHILLIPS & CO.

Wholesale and Retail Dealers in

# BOOTS, SHOES

### LEATHER AND SHOE FINDINGS,

Farnham Street, Omaha, N. T.     Broadway, Council Bluffs, Iowa.

A Large Assortment of **PIKE'S PEAK BOOTS**.

☞ CASH PAID FOR HIDES AND FURS. ☜

---

# HARDWARE!

## CHAS. J. FOX,

Wholesale and Retail Dealer in

### AMERICAN, ENGLISH and GERMAN

# HARDWARE AND CUTLERY,

Iron, Steel, Nails, Glass, Saws, Guns, Rifles, Pistols and Agricultural Implements,

GENERAL OUTFITTING HARDWARE HOUSE FOR CALIFORNIA AND PIKE'S PEAK TRADE.

Sign of the Gilt Plow, Council Bluffs, Iowa.

---

## BEERS & CO.

WHOLESALE AND RETAIL DEALERS IN

# GROCERIES, PROVISIONS,

—AND—

## OUTFITTING GOODS.

☞ Special attention paid to Pike's Peak, Salt Lake California and Oregon Emigrant Trade. A large quantity of BACON, FLOUR, etc., constantly on hand.

**THE LARGEST EXCLUSIVE GROCERY AND OUTFITTING HOUSE**

IN THE CITY.

COUNCIL BLUFFS, IOWA,

---

J. POUDRE.                E. E. SANBORN.

## CENTRAL MARKET.

### POUDRE & SANBORN,

Wholesale and Retail Dealers in

# FRESH, SALT AND DRIED MEATS,

Beef, Mutton and Pork,

**MIDDLE BROADWAY,**  - - -  **COUNCIL BLUFFS, IOWA.**

Particular attention paid to putting up Dried Meats, Bologne Sausage and every thing in our line, that is needed for the Pike's Peak Trade. Steamboats and Hotels supplied on reasonable terms.

# FARMERS' HOTEL

### J. D. CLUFF, Proprietor,

Middle Broadway, - - Council Bluffs.

---

This House is centrally located, the accommodations are good, and charges reasonable.

**GOOD STABLING CONNECTED WITH THE HOUSE.**

---

# CITY HOTEL,

### Middle Broadway, Council Bluffs, Ioaa,

### HIRAM SHOEMAKER, - - PROPRIETOR.

Travelers will find it convenient to take the Stage at the City Hotel for all points North, South, East and West.

**BOARD $1 PER DAY, or $3.50 PER WEEK.**

GOOD STABLING CONNECTED TO THE HOTEL.

---

### G. Th. MUELLER,

MANUFACTURER AND DEALER IN

# Tobacco, Cigars and Snuff,

VIRGINIA TOBACCO AND FANCY PIPES,

Lower Broadway, opposite the County Judge's Office,

COUNCIL BLUFFS, IOWA.

---

### S. McFADDEN,

# LIVERY, FEED

—AND—

## SALE STABLE,

MIDDLE BROADWAY,

COUNCIL BLUFFS, IOWA.

## PLATTSMOUTH, NEBRASKA,

Is situated a short distance from the mouth of the Platte. It has several large outfitting house. A good steam ferry makes trips every ten minutes across the Missouri river. The road from here to Fort Kearney is good, and the distance shorter than from any other starting point. Your attention is called to the following advertisements.

---

## SPRATLEN, DAVIS & CO.,
### WHOLESALE DEALERS IN
# DRY GOODS,
## GROCERIES,
## Boots and Shoes, Hardware
## BACON, FLOUR,
—AND—
## ALL KINDS OF OUTFITTING GOODS.
### IN THE LARGE BRICK STORE,
### CORNER MAIN AND SIXTH STREETS,
### PLATTSMOUTH, • • • • • NEBRASKA.

T. E. TOOTLE.         T. K. HANNA.

## TOOTLE & HANNA,
### DEALERS IN
# DRY GOODS, GROCERIES
## BOOTS AND SHOES, HARDWARE,
## BACON, FLOUR
—AND—
## ALL KINDS OF OUTFITTING GOODS.
—ALSO—
### Commission and Forwarding Merchants.
### CORNER MAIN STREET AND LEVEE,
### PLATTSMOUTH, - - NEBRASKA.

# THE PLACE TO PROCURE OUTFITS
## AT THE NEW BRICK STORE.

### JOHN W. MARSHALL,
DEALER IN

### Flour, Meal, Bacon, Sugar, Tea, Coffee,
TOBACCO, DRIED FRUIT, RICE, CRACKERS,

## CLOTHING, BOOTS, SHOES,
And, indeed, EVERYTHING USUALLY KEPT IN A DRY GOODS ESTABLISHMENT.
Call and see for yourselves.

**BRICK BUILDING ON MAIN STREET, near the Levee,**
**PLATTSMOUTH, NEBRASKA.**

---

## CITY MEAT MARKET,
GOTTFRED FICKLER, Proprietor.

All kinds of SAUSAGES, DRIED and PRESERVED MEATS on hand put up to order.

**PLATTSMOUTH, NEBRASKA.**

---

AUGUSTUS RHEINHACKEL,
Manufacturer and Dealer in

## ALL KINDS OF HARNESS,
Plattsmouth, Nebraska.

ALL KINDS OF REPAIRING DONE.

---

### JOHN WAHL,
## MERCHANT TAILOR,
PLATTSMOUTH, - - - NEBRASKA.

☞ All kinds of Tailoring and Repairing done on short notice.

---

### HAYS & GOFF,
## BAKERY AND GROCERY,
PLATTSMOUTH, - - - - - - NEBRASKA.

## NEBRASKA CITY, N. T.,

Is situated on the west side of the Missouri river; it possesses superior facilities as an outfitting and starting point for Pike's Peak. A new road has lately been laid out by A. Majors, Nuckolls & Hawke and a number of heavy freighters across the Plains, by which the distance is greatly shortened to Fort Kearney. Settlements are thick a large portion of the distance, and ranches, farms and stations can be found at convenient distances; wood, water and grass can be had in abundance; corn, hay and oats may be purchased at reasonable rates. The country around Nebraska City being thickly settled, cattle and stock are plenty and are sold at reasonable prices. A first class steam ferry is in readiness at all times to carry passengers and teams, at reduced rates of ferriage. A large number of the heavy freighters make this their starting point.

Before making purchases or transacting business at any other place, the emigrant should first call on the firms whose advertisements appear herewith. Having special facilities for meeting the wants of those that may call on them, they desire to let the public know of it.

## DISTANCES FROM NEBRASKA CITY TO FORT KEARNEY.

|  | MILES. |  |
|---|---|---|
| WILSON'S BRIDGE.—Settlement. Hay, grain, water, grass and timber abundant................................................... | 9 |  |
| BROWNELL'S BRIDGE.—Blacksmith shop; good camping ground, etc................................................................. | 7 | 16 |
| BRIDGE OVER LITTLE NEMAHA.—Settlers all along the route; abundance of everything required by the emigrant........ | 4 | 20 |
| HEAD OF LITTLE NEMAHA.—Settled all along; good camping ground; plenty of water, wood and grass................. | 20 | 40 |
| OLATHA.—Small town, has been settled for four years. Corn, hay, and everything required by the emigrant, in abundance..... | 8 | 48 |
| BERANGER—at East Fork of Blue. Large settlement of French; Vifquain's trading post; good camping ground............ | 18 | 66 |
| GROVE OF TIMBER.—Plenty of timber, grass and water.... | 15 | 81 |
| HEAD OF NORTH FORK OF BLUE RIVER.—From here, for 50 miles, the road runs parallel with the Blue River, and not more than three miles from it at any place. There are a few settlers along this road, and abundance of timber, water and grass all along the route................................................... | 48 | 129 |

| | | MLS. |
|---|---|---|
| A POND—a little south of the road; good camping ground... | 5 | 134 |
| PRAIRIE LAKE.—Good timber, water and grass................ | 8 | 142 |
| JUNCTION—Platte river and old California road. Ranche and station; good wood, water, grass and camping ground........ | 5 | 147 |
| FORT KEARNEY.—Good wood, water and grass. Fort Kearney is 1¼ miles south of a due west line from Nebraska City, according to the Government Surveys, as can be seen by referring to a reliable map just published by authority of the Government. Fort Kearney is 168 miles west from Nebraska City on an air line............................................................................... | 80 | 177 |

---

DWIGHT J. McCANN.                                                                     JULIAN METCALF.

# M'CANN & METCALF,

# BANKERS,

# DEALERS IN GOLD DUST,

## *Gold and Silver Coin,*

### Uncurrent Money, Land Warrants and Exchange.

NEBRASKA CITY,    :    :    :    :    NEBRASKA.

---

Will receive Gold Dust and forward to the United States Mint for assay; will make liberal advances on the same, and remit for balance, as soon as we receive the Mint certificate, in exchange on New York, Philadelphia or St. Louis, available in any part of the Union.

Collections made in this city and vicinity, and remitted for promptly at current rates of Exchange. Taxes paid for non-residents, and all business intrusted to our care will receive prompt and accurate attention, and at reasonable charges.

---

We Refer to our Correspondents:

HOFFMAN & CO., New York.
DREXEL & CO., Philadelphia.
HARROLD, WILLIAMS & CO., Philadelphia.
UNION BANKING CO., Pittsburgh.
F. G. ADAMS, Chicago.

GILMORE, DUNLAP & CO. Cincinnati.
A. M. PERRY & CO., Cleveland.
ALLEN, COPP & NESBET, St. Louis.
WESTERN BANK, St. Joseph.
S. G. THOMPSON, Assayer U. S. Mint.

ALEX. MAJORS, Nebraska City and Denver.
SWEENY, RITTENHOUSE, FANT & CO., Washington.

# BANKING HOUSE
—OF—
## J. A. WARE,
NEBRASKA CITY, – – NEBRASKA.

Coin, Gold Dust, Exchange and Uncurrent Bank Notes
BOUGHT AND SOLD.

REFER TO—STATE SAVING ASSOCIATION, St. Louis, Mo.; ALEX. MAJORS, Kansas City Mo.; READ, DREXEL & CO., New York; DREXEL & CO., Philadelpia, Penn.

## N. S. HARDIN & CO'S
## NEWS DEPOT,
IN THE POST OFFICE,
### NEBRASKA CITY, N. T.
Dealers in Books, Stationery, Magazines and Newspapers.

Always on hand the latest dates of the leading New York, Chicago, St. Louis and Cincinnati daily and weekly newspapers.

Illustrated Papers—Frank Leslie's, Harper's Weekly, New York Illustrated News and Gleason's Pictorial. All the principal Literary papers, such as—New York Ledger, Mercury, Weekly, Flag of our Union, Saturday Evening Post, Home Journal, Saturday Press; together with all the leading Monthly Magazines, American, English and German Papers, Novels, Books and Stationery; all for sale at Publishers' Prices. Call and get something to read before starting over the Plains. REMEMBER! at the Post Office.

N. S. HARDIN & CO.

## ST. LOUIS BAKERY.
ALWAYS ON HAND A LARGE ASSORTMENT OF
### BREAD, CRACKERS, PILOT BREAD, CAKES
### AND PIES,
Put up in quanties for the Pike's Peak trade, by

**KLOENE & SCHMIDT,**
MAIN ST., NEBRASKA CITY, N. T.

## PENNSYLVANIA BLACKSMITH SHOP.

Blacksmithing of all kinds done with neatness and dispatch.

Repairing done on short notice and on reasonable terms.

MARTIN SHACKLER, Proprietor,
Main Street, Nebraska City.

## ST. LOUIS STORE.

### KALKMAN & WESSELS,

CORNER OF THIRD STREET AND FRANKLIN AVENUE,

NEBRASKA CITY. Nebraska Territory,

A large and complete stock of

## DRY GOODS,
## GROCERIES AND PROVISIONS,

### QUEENSWARE,

### HATS AND CAPS, BOOTS, SHOES,

And a general assortment of

## OUTFITTING GOODS,

And every variety of articles usually kept in a

### WESTERN STORE.

We are prepared to SELL LOWER than any other House West of the Mississippi River, being a branch of the firm of Kalkman & Wessels, St. Louis.

☞ ALL GOODS WARRANTED TO BE AS RECOMMENDED. ☜

**ONE PRICE, AND NO CREDIT.**

## BUETER & CO.,

# GENERAL OUTFITTING DEPOT

Between Franklin Avenue and Third Street,

## NEBRASKA CITY, - - NEBRASKA.

We have for sale the largest and best selected Stock of

## GROCERIES, PROVISIONS,

## DRY GOODS,

## BOOTS AND SHOES, HATS AND CAPS,

## Hardware, Queensware, Glass, Glassware,

## DRUGS and NAILS,

All of which we will sell at the

## LOWEST MARKET PRICES!

### FOR CASH OR COUNTRY PRODUCE,

TO THE

## WHOLESALE AND RETAIL TRADE.

### BUETER & CO.

## GOODLETT & GREGG,
#### WHOLESALE AND RETAIL DEALERS IN
## STOVES, TINWARE AND HARDWARE,
##### CONSISTING IN PART OF
#### SHEET IRON STOVES, GOLD WASHERS,
### CAMP KETTLES, COFFEE BOILERS, COOK & HEATING STOVES,
Of the Best and most Approved Designs.

### CALL AND SEE FOR YOURSELVES.
#### NEBRASKA CITY.

## HAWKE & NUCKOLLS,
#### WHOLESALE AND RETAIL DEALERS IN

## HARDWARE,
### HATS, CAPS, BOOTS, SHOES, CLOTHING,
#### Glass and China Ware, Iron, Nails,
## CASTINGS, SHEET COPPER, STEEL,
### FLOUR, BACON, GROCERIES,
—AND—
## MINERS' GOODS GENERALLY,
#### NEBRASKA CITY, NEBRASKA TERRITORY.

Also, A GOOD ASSORTMENT OF CHOICE LIQUORS.

## CITY MEAT MARKET
### ALL KINDS OF
## Sausage, Fresh, Dried, Preserved and other Meats,
#### Especially adapted to the Pike's Peak Trade.
### CHARLES GERBER,
#### Main Street, Nebraska City, N. T.

## OUTFITTING AND TRANSPORTATION.

## NEBRASKA CITY AND PIKE'S PEAK
# TRANSPORTATION LINE.

### ALEXANDER MAJORS,
# GENERAL FREIGHTER
#### TO THE MINES,

Is prepored to forward any amount of Freight from Nebraska City, N. T. to Denver City and the Towns and Mines of the Pike's Peak Gold Regions generally. Having made extensive preparations, and from his long experience in the freighting business, he can offer unusual facilities for the prompt and speedy transportation of Freight to the Mines at reasonable rates.

All goods shipped to his care, destined for the Mines, will be stored properly, without any charge for receiving or storage. He is also prepared to furnish emigrants with

**COMPLETE OUTFITS FOR THE MINES.**

# WAGONS, OX-YOKES, CHAINS,

Picks, Axes, Cordage, Camp Kit,

**CLOTHING, BOOTS, SHOES, HATS, CAPS,**

and GROCERIES of all kinds,

Purchased in large quantities, for his Transportation and Outfitting business. He has also

**BLACKSMITH and WAGON SHOPS on the Premises,**

and capacious private grounds for corralling Stock, at his

OUTFIT STORE, IN WEST NEBRASKA CITY.

# D. B. McMECHAN,

Wholesale and Retail Dealer in

# HARDWARE, CUTLERY,

### SADDLERS' HARDWARE, IRON, NAILS, CASTINGS,
## STOVES AND TINWARE.

Has always on hand a large and complete Stock of everything belonging to this business, and of the best quality, such as

Hunt, Simmons & Collin's Axes, Picks, Mattocks and Edge Tools. Spades and Shovels of "Ames'" and other make. Crow Bars. Drills, Log, Coil, Trace, Fifth, Back, Dog and Halter Chains. Rope of all Sizes. Also, Sheet Iron for Toms, Sheet Iron Cook Stoves, Camp Kettles, Gold Pans, Tin and Sheet Iron.

In short everything required by the emigrant for a complete outfit for Camping and Mining, which I will sell to emigrants and others at a small advance on Eastern Prices.

I am prepared to do Sheet Iron, Copper or Tin work of any kind, at short notice.

☛ I will send a Price List of things required for an outfit, free of postage, to any one requesting it.

**Sign of the Big Padlock, corner Franklin Avenue and Third St., Nebraska City.**

---

# R. M. ROLFE & CO.

Wholesale and Retail Dealers in

## GROCERIES, LIQUORS,
### CIGARS,
## FLOUR, MEAL, PORK, BACON, ETC.

Outfitters for the Mountains will find it to their advantage to give this House a call before purchasing elsewhere.

**KEARNEY WARD, NEBRASKA CITY, N. T.**

---

# PLANTERS' HOUSE,

### W. P. BIRCHFIELD, Proprietor.

## CORNER OF FRONT AND COMMERCIAL STREETS,
### NEBRASKA CITY, N. T.

**GOOD STABLING IN CONNECTION WITH THIS HOUSE.**

## A. ALBRIGHT,
### MANUFACTURER OF
# BOOTS AND SHOES
### Main Street, Nebraska City.

**CASH PAID FOR HIDES.**

---

T. ASHTON.  J. N. TAIT.

## ASHTON & TAIT,
### Forwarding and Commission Merchants,
#### STEAM BOAT AGENTS,
##### DEALERS IN
### DRY GOODS, GROCERIES, PROVISIONS & OUTFITTING GOODS.

Emigrants to the Gold Mines will find it to their advantage to ship to our care, as we are convenient to the Steamboat Landing, and have ample room for Storage. Give us a trial. Charges moderate.

**On the Levee, Nebraska City, N. T.**

ASHTON & TAIT.

REFER TO—Hannibal & St. Joseph Railroad Company.

---

### Guns, Pistols and Bowie Knives.

## WILLIAM ROTTON,
#### Manufacturer and Dealer in all kinds of
# RIFLES, SHOT-GUNS, PISTOLS, &c.

Would respectfully inform all Sportsmen and the inhabitants of Nebraska City and surrounding country, that he has on hand, and will continue to keep the largest assortment of Double and Single Barreled Guns; Pistols of every description, together with all kinds of Amunition. Also, Ely's Wadding. Cartridges and Caps; Powder of the best brands, Shot and Bullet Pouches and Powder Flasks of all sizes can be purchased at all times from his extensive stock. Target and Sporting Rifles made to order.

☞ SHOP, ON MAIN STREET, two doors west of the Morton House.
☞ Repairing done neatly and promptly.

---

### OPPOSITION TO THE WORLD AT
## SEIGEL, GREENBAUM & CO'S,
MAIN STREET, OPPOSITE MORTON HOUSE, - - NEBRASKA CITY.

### FALL AND WINTER
# CLOTHING!
**BOOTS, SHOES, HATS, CAPS, FURNISHING GOODS, FANCY GOODS, CARPET BAGS, and GUM OVERCOATS, OVERALLS AND BOOTS,**

Cheaper than ever before known in the West, just opened at the Baltimore Clothing Depot of SEIGEL, GREENEBAUM & Co.

## WHITNIGER & WARREN,

DEALERS IN

# DRUGS, CHEMICALS,

### Perfumery, Dye Stuffs, Paints, Oils,

Fancy Articles, Patent Medicines, Books, Paper, Envelopes, Fine Tobacco, Cigars and Good Liquors.

☞ All articles genuine and of extra quality. Prices low for Cash.

### MAIN STREET, NEBRASKA CITY.

## SIMON & SEEMAN,

WHOLESALE AND RETAIL DEALERS IN

# CIGARS,  TOBACCO

### All kinds of PIPES, PLAYING CARDS, ETC.

ALSO, AGENTS FOR

**J. M. BRUNSWICK & BRO., Billiard Table Manufacturers.**

Constantly on hand, an assortment of

### BILLIARD TABLES, CUES, CUE LEATHERS, ETC.

### LEAVENWORTH CITY, KANSAS.

Branch Store, under the style and firm of SIMON, SEEMAN & CO., conducted by Mr. J. S. HERMAN,

### DENVER CITY, ROCKY MOUNTAINS.

## P. W. GATES & CO'S
# PATENT QUARTZ MILLS.

We have made some very important improvements upon the Mills manufactured by us last year, but our increased facilities for manufacturing, and the anticipation of a large trade from Pike's Peak, will enable us to sell our mills, with all the additional improvements at less price than last year. Our **Patent Chilled Shoes and Dies** make our mills worth to wear out double any other stamp mill now in use, and our experience in the best plan for collecting and saving the gold dust, will give parties purchasing from us a decided advantage over those buying of other manufacturers.

CAMS AND COLLARS.—The face of our Cams and Collars will be chilled, and will last many years; and their peculiar form give them a decided preference over any others in use.

ADJUSTABLE COLLARS.—Our Collars are put on with a screw and key, and cannot get loose. When the Shoe wears off, the Collar can be changed to give the proper lift—a great improvement over Stamps that have the Collars solid or immovable.

REVOLVING STAMPS.—Our Stamps revolve. This saves power and causes the Shoe to wear equal—a great advantage over the ordinary plan.

As there are many who have not the means to pay for a first-class mill, we purpose to furnish a cheaper mill to run either by steam or water power, with our PATENT CHILLED SHOES and Heads for stamps with Wood Stems.

We repeat the advice so often given last season—let experiments alone, and when you purchase, take the stamps which have outlived all the *Coffee Mills* and humbugs that have ever been introduced.

Our *Patent Chilled Shoes and Dies* are warranted to be chilled entirely through. We furnish Pulverizers to go with our Stamps, if wanted; either the Chilian mill or our own patent pulverizer.

RETORTS kept on hand. PUMPS for the mines of any capacity.

Price of Stamp Mills is governed by the number and size of Stamps wanted. For particulars, address us by mail, naming the size and number of Stamps, which will receive a prompt reply.

THE SIZE OF OUR STAMP MILLS ARE AS FOLLOWS:

| No. 1—weight of Stamps, | 300 pounds each. | No. 5—weight of Stamps, | 700 pounds each. |
|---|---|---|---|
| " 2 " | " 400 " | " 6 " | " 800 " |
| " 3 " | " 500 " | " 7 " | " 900 " |
| " 4 " | " 600 " | " 8 " | " 1000 " |

CAUTION.—We caution all persons against buying stamps of manufacturers who profess to furnish *Chilled Shoes and Dies*, as Shoes cannot be *chilled*, to be of any service, except by a process we have patented, and any person infringing on our rights, either by making or using our *Chilled Shoes and Dies*, must answer at a court of justice.

P. W. GATES & CO'S PORTABLE ENGINES, from Five to Sixteen Horse Power.

STATIONARY ENGINES, from Five to Five Hundred Horse Power. Also, Boilers for same, either Tubular, Locomotive, or the ordinary two-flued Boilers.

Portable Circular Saw Mills, Superior Shingle Mills, Portable Flour and Corn Mills, Corn Shellers, Mill Gearing, Sugar Cane Mills and Evaporators, Engine Trimmings, Steam Gauges, Brass Work, and all kinds of Machinery.

We have sold about sixty Mills, and refer parties at the mountains, who wish to purchase, to the following gentlemen. Many of them own and are running our mills, and all are practical men and have examined our mills and machinery.

**P. W. GATES & CO.**
**EAGLE WORKS, CHICAGO, ILL.**

C. WILTSE, Correspondent R. Mountain News.
R. PACKARD.
JOHN H. GREGORY.
HARRY GUNNELL, Discoverer Gunnell Lead.
T. T. PROSSER.
B. W. CROUCH, Proprietor of late Colman & LeFever's Mill, made at St. Louis, and Practical Miner on Gunnell's Lead.
JOSEPH B. COFIELD, Nevada Gulch.
J. H. RICE, " "
E. LAWRENCE, " "
J. HEDGES, " "
F. R. FORD, " "
H. B. BEARCE, " "
H. F. PARKER, Sup't Lawrence Mining Co.
JOSEPH CASTO, of the Casto Lead, and P. M. of Mountain City.

GEO. W. BRIZEE, Attorney at Law.
A. C. SWIFT, California and Australia Miner.
CHAS. H. SIMMONS.
CHAS. W. FISK, Discoverer of Fisk Lead.
WM. H. BATES, of Bates' Lead.
O. F. BARKER, Geologist and Assayer of Quartz Rock.
TAYLOR, GRISWOLD & CO., Mountain City.
C. S. ABBOTT, Sec. Am. Mining Co., "
MOSES BUTTERWORTH & CO., "
CRANE & BOYD, Eureka Gulch.
R. W. CRAMPTON, Sup't C., B. & Q. Quartz Mining Co., Nevada City.
R. W. CLARK & CO., Eureka, Gregory Mines.
V. B. BELL, Secretary Chicago Mutual Mining Company, Russel's Gulch.

## OUTFITTING & TRANSPORTATION.

### NEBRASKA CITY AND PIKE'S PEAK
# *TRANSPORTATION*
## LINE.

## A. & P. BYRAM,

(Successors to Alexander Majors,)

## GENERAL FREIGHTERS to MINES,

Are prepared to forward any amount of Freight from Nebraska City, N. T. to Denver City and the Towns and Mines of the Pike's Peak Gold Regions generally. Having made extensive preparations, from our long experience in the freighting business, we can offer unusual facilities for the prompt and speedy transportation of Freight to the Mines at reasonable rates.

All goods shipped to our care, destined for the Mines, will be stored properly, without any charge for receiving or storage. We are also prepared to furnish emigrants with

*COMPLETE OUTFITS FOR THE MINES.*

## WAGONS, OX-YOKES, CHAINS, PICKS, AXES, CORDAGE,

CAMP KIT, CLOTHING, BOOTS, SHOES,

Hats, Caps, and Groceries of all kinds,

Purchased in large quantities, for our Transportation and Outfitting business. We have also

**BLACKSMITH and WAGON SHOPS** on the premises,

and capacious private grounds for corralling Stock, at our

OUTFIT STORE IN WEST NEBRASKA CITY.

## UNITED STATES MAIL COACH TO DENVER!

### J. H. ANDREWS,
## DEALER IN HARNESS, SADDLES, BRIDLES, WHIPS,

AND everything usually found in a Saddler's establishment. He would call particular attention to a new SCOTCH COLLAR, which supercedes all others, and is now being generally used, either for team work or light buggy harness. We would also say that this collar is manufactured by no other establishment on the Missouri Slope. His prices wil be uniformly low for cash. He has a large stock of

### LEATHER AND SADDLERY,

which he will sell to the wholesale trade at St. Louis rates, adding transportation.

Shops, on Douglas street, opposite the Tremont House, and on Farnham street, a few doors east of Megeath's store. Our Collars are warranted not to rub or chafe a horse.

OMAHA, NEBRASKA.

---

### COOLIDGE & WHEELER,
#### WHOLESALE & RETAIL DEALERS IN

### Stoves, Tinware, Cooking Stoves, of every Size & Style,

Camp Stoves, of several varieties on hand, Camp Kettles, Plates, Cups, Pans, Canteens, Cans, and in fact every thing the Miner can wish or ask for in our line, will be kept on hand and sold as cheap as at any Point on the Missouri River. We also keep a good supply of Copper and Sheet Iron of different kinds and qualities, to suit all.

PLATTSMOUTH, NEBRASKA.

---

# JEFFERSON HOUSE!

### W. H. PILES, Proprietor.

Ferry Street, Between Third & Fourth,

### DENVER CITY.

---

# IOWA HOUSE,

### J. F. SMITH, Proprietor.

CHERRY STREET, NEAR FERRY STREET BRIDGE,

### DENVER CITY.

# DENVER
## TOBACCO and CIGAR
# EMPORIUM,

### CORNER BLAKE & F STREETS,

(ESTABLISHED MAY 1859.)

### H. J. BRENDLINGER, Pro.

In this establishment will be found the

### LARGEST, MOST VARIED, & BEST SELECTED

STOCK OF

## TOBACCO and CIGARS,

Together with all articles pertaining to the business, to be found in the whole Pike's Peak Region, and the prices, the lowest. My stock comprises the finest selection of CHEWING TOBACCO'S of every grade and quality of NATURAL LEAF, Sweet and Plain, any variety of Fancy Brands. Also FINE CUT in bulk and packages. CIGARS, direct from Havana, of the most fragrant qualities, together with a general stock of all other descriptions, of all grades Smoking Tobacco, in barrels, bales, papers and other styles. PIPES, the finest MEERSCHAUM, also the different kinds kept in any other market. PLAYING CARDS, of the various kinds, also a complete assortment of Matches, fancy and ordinary, and numbers of articles usually kept in a first class Tobacco and Cigar establishment, not here enumerated. I would respectfully call the attention of the local and mountain trade, and persons visiting Denver to my stock of goods, which for variety, quality and general excellence cannot be surpassed and for prices the most reasonable.

# PLATTE HOUSE!

Blake Street, bet. E. F. sts.

## GENERAL STAGE OFFICE

C. O. C. & P. P. E. CO.

M. V. B. ROLLiNS, : Proprietor.

DENVER CITY, J. T.

---

G. W. CLAYTON,

— DEALER IN —

*Groceries, Dry Goods!*

CLOTHING, BOOTS, SHOES, and

GOODS OF EVERY DESCRIPTION.

CORNER OF LARIMER and F sts.,

DENVER CITY.

---

J. M. IDDINGS & CO.,

STORAGE AND COMMISS'N MERCH'TS,

FERRY STREET, Above Fifth.

DENVER CITY, J. T.

☞ Consignments Solicited.

---

PIONEER STABLE.

JOHN WANLESS,

LIVERY & FEED STABLE,

CORNER FOURTH and CHERRY STS.,

DENVER CITY.

I am prepared to keep an unlimited number of stock, at all times, either in stable or on best ranch in this country. Also, Drays and first class Livery stock, at reasonable rates.

GUIDE TO THE GOLD MINES.

# JACOB BLATTNER,

MANUFACTURER AND IMPORTER OF

## GOLD SCALES AND WEIGHTS!

**RETORTS and MAGNETS,**

Microscopes and Pocket Compases,

SPY GLASSES,

THERMOMETERS, BAROMETERS, SURVEYOR'S COMPASSES
AND LEVELLING INSTRUMENTS,

No. 44, Market Street, St. Louis, Mo.

---

Make Way for the Mammoth Stock.

WM. RUTH

IS NOW IN RECEIPT OF HIS

## IMMENSE STOCK OF DRY-GOODS

FOR THE SPRING TRADE.

**LARGER STOCK AND LOWER PRICES THAN EVER.**

THE ONLY EXCLUSIVE WHOLESALE AND RETAIL DRY GOOD HOUSE IN OMAHA. REMEMBER THE PLACE—PIONEER BLOCK, FARNHAM ST.

WM. RUTH, thankful for past favors, would again call the attention of the citizens of Omaha and surrounding country, to the fact that he has now ready for inspection an immense stock of Dry Goods. An attempt to enumerate would be fruitless. His stock consists in part of the following line of goods:

Sheetings, Shirtings, Denims, Ticks, Carpets, Bleached Goods, Cloths, Cassimeres, Satinetts, Jeans, Cottonades, Linens, Prints, Ginghams, Lawns, Delaines, Barages, Organdies. I would call the attention of the ladies particularly to my line of DRESS GOODS, as I am confident they are unequalled in variety of style, beauty and fabric. Dress trimmings, in great variety, Bonnets, Ornaments, Parsols, Ribbons, Laces, Hoop Skirts, Shawls, Head Dresses, Embroideries, Gloves and Hosiery, and an endless stock of Yankee Notions. Also, men's and boy's Hats and Caps, Ready-Made Clothing, Shirts, Drawers, &c., &c. Garments manufactured to order.

N. B. The Ready Pay System will be adhered to. My motto is

**QUICK SALES AND SMALL PROFITS.**

## J. F. SCHMELZER,

MANUFACTURER AND DEALER IN

# Guns, Rifles and Pistols.

### ALL KINDS OF

## SPORTING APPARATUS.

### No. 35, Delaware Street, bet. 2d and 3d,

#### LEAVENWORTH, KANSAS.

Persons going to the Gold Mines should call and see. All kinds of Arms made to order and repaired on short notice in workmanlike manner.

---

## J. P. BLACK & CO.,

WHOLESALE & RETAIL DEALERS IN

# STOVES & TINWARE!

### ALL KINDS OF

## Brass, Copper and Sheet Iron Ware,

Opposite **Tremont House,**
Douglas Street, } **OMAHA, N. T.**

We have on hand a fine assortment of

- Cast Iron Stoves,
- Sheet Iron Stoves,
- Tinware of all kinds,
- Japanned Ware,
- French Ware,
- Camp Kettles,
- Porcelain Kettles,
- Brass Kettles,
- Dutch Ovens,
- Fry Pans,
- Skillets,
- Coffee Mills,
- Iron Spoons,
- Tinned Sauce Pans.

We manufacture Enamelled Plates, and keep constantly on hand the best style of Camp Stoves used on the Plains.

---

## HEISEL & VALLEREY,
## STEAM FLOURING MILL,
### PLATTSMOUTH, N. T.

**K**EEP constantly on hand the best Brands of Flour. Emigrants will please call before purchasing elsewhere.

---

## DR. W. E. DONELAN,
— DEALER IN —

### Drugs, Medicines, Chemicals, Paints, Oils, Perfumery,

Patent Medicines and Fancy Goods.

PLATTSMOUTH, - - - NEBRASKA.

# COLORADO TERRITORY.

Since the publication of our first edition of this book, a Bill has passed the House of Representatives for the temporary government of this country. Although its name has been changed according to law, we will venture to predict that the original appellation of "Pike's Peak" will be the name by which it will be known, as long as that "*venerated*" mountain continues to greet the eye of the "*Pilgrim*," when on his way to the modern ophir.

The following are the most prominent features of the Bill, passed 7th February, 1861.

*Boundaries.*—Commencing on the 37th parallel of North latitude, where the 25th meredian of longitude West from Washington crosses the same, thence North on said meredian to the forty-first parallel of North latitude, thence along said parellel, West to the 32nd meredian of longitude West from Washington, thence South on said meredian to the Northern Line of New Mexico, thence along the 37th parellel of North latitude to the place of begining.

*General Laws.*—The Governor of the Territory is vested with the powers of Commander-in-Chief of the Militia and Superintendent of Indian Affairs; he has power of appointing and removing all officers holding office under the laws of said Territory. All Legislative power is vested in the Governor and Legislative Assembly which consists of a Council and House of Representatives—Council consists of nine members, and may be increased to thirteen; the House consists of thirteen members, and may be increased to 26.

The Federal power of the Territory is vested in a Supreme Court. District Courts, Probate Courts and Justices of the Peace.

The Governor, Secretary, Chief Justice and Associate Justices, Attorney and Marshal are nominated by and with the advice and consent of the Senate, and are appointed by the President of the United States.

*Salaries.*—Governor, 1,300 annually, and one thousand dollars as Superintendent of Indian Affairs. Chief and Associate Judges and Secretary, $1,800 per annum. Members of the Legislature, $3,00 per day, and $3,00 for every twenty miles travelled when going to and returning from the seat of government.

We are provided with one delegate to the House of Representatives of the United States, he is elected by popular vote. Sections 16 and 36 in each Township are reserved for school purposes.

The President of the United States has power to appoint a Surveyor for the Territory.

# CORRECTIONS, NOTICES, &C., &C.

**WESTERN FOUNDRY, ST. LOUIS.**—In estimating the number of Quartz Mills, Stamps, &c., (on page 52,) manufactured by the several foundries, we stated in our first edition, that E. C. Totten & Co. had manufactured 122 Stamps, we have just been informed by Mr. Totten that his establishment has manufactured 189 Stamps—we would here remind our readers that this firm are the exclusive manufacturers of the solid steel faced Stamps, which is giving universal satisfaction amongst all the Quartz Mills that are using them.

**NEBRASKA CITY, N. T.**—On our map of routes (by an oversight) we did not notice the Burlington and Missouri Railroad, from Burlington and Keokuk to Nebraska City. The roads are now completed to Ottumwa. Emigrants coming from the East or Mississippi River can start from either Burlington or Keokuk, take the railroad to Ottumwa, and from thence a line of stages run in connection with the railroad to carry passengers to Nebraska City, via Clarinda, at reduced rates.

A. P. BYRAM & Co., successors to Alex. Majors, have taken charge of the latter gentleman's extensive freighting business. They are now prepared to carry freight of any amount, from Nebraska City to all points throughout the mines. See their advertisement.

WHITINGER & WARREN, Druggists, have dissolved partnership. The business will be carried on as formerly, by Mr. D. Whitinger.

EMIGRANTS should remember that the "*Live Book Store*" of N. S. Harding & Co., in the Post Office, is the only place where they can obtain all the latest papers, best periodicals and novels, and enumerable quantities and styles of stationery. Exclusive wholesale and retail Agents in Nebraska City for this Guide.

**OMAHA, N. T.**—By a mistake of the Lithographer the railroad from Rock Island and Davenport to Council Bluffs and Omaha, is made to show a continuous and complete running line to the latter place; the railroad is now running to Marengo, and from thence the Western Stage Company, run a daily line conveying passengers to Council Bluffs and Omaha. Time from Chicago to Omaha by this road, 34 hours.

EMIGRANTS and others designing a trip across the plains should not forget to pay the "News Depot" of B. P. Graves a visit; they will here find a choice and select assortment of Books, newspapers, periodicals, novels, and all kinds of stationery. Orders received and filled for all the popular American, English, German and Irish newspapers and magazines at club rates. Exclusive Agents in Omaha for the Rocky Mountain Gold Regions and Emigrants Guide.

**MONTANA DISTRICT.**—We have just been shown by Mr. T. C. Willard a specimen of Gold bearing Quartz, taken out of one of Mr. Frank Bourke's claims, which he is now opening. In richness it surpasses anything that we have yet seen. Small ingots of gold is discernable with the naked eye, scattered promiscuously all over. Mr. Bourke asserts that the pay dirt averages 35 cents to the pan. Several Quartz Mills are being located here, and will be in active operation as soon as the machinery can be put up. The following are the names of the regularly appointed officers. E. P. Peters, President. T. C. Willard, Recorder. Thomas Kennon, Judge. Hon. G. W. Purkins, District Attorney. Charles Collins, Inspector of Claims and Boundaries.

---

# HUGHES HOUSE.

## H. M. HUGHES, Proprietor.

### CORNER COMMERCIAL AND SIXTH STREET
### ATCHISON, KANSAS.

*Omnibus and Baggage Wagons always in readiness to convey passengers or baggage to and from steamboats and cars.*

A good Livery Stable connected with the House. ☞ Stages leave daily for all the principal points in the interior.

www.ingramcontent.com/pod-product-compliance
Lightning Source LLC
Chambersburg PA
CBHW022131160426
43197CB00009B/1233